for David

happy XXXIII

John

GW00643213

TWO
VICTORIAN FAMILIES

TWO VICTORIAN FAMILIES

By

BETTY ASKWITH

1973

CHATTO & WINDUS

LONDON

Published by
Chatto & Windus Ltd.
40/42 William IV Street
London W.C.2

*

Clark, Irwin and Co., Ltd.
Toronto

First published 1971
Second impression 1973

ISBN 0 7011 1804 0

© Betty Askwith 1971

Printed in Great Britain by
Redwood Press Limited
Trowbridge, Wiltshire

CONTENTS

PLATES

ACKNOWLEDGEMENTS

I should like to express my gratitude to the Strachey Trust for allowing me to borrow the family letters and papers on which the first part of this book is so largely based. In particular I should like to thank Lucy Norton, whose idea it was that I should undertake this work, who provided so much information, support and encouragement, and who introduced me to Mrs James Strachey, to Duncan Grant, to Quentin Bell and Michael Holroyd, who were all extremely helpful. I am especially indebted to Duncan Grant for his fascinating first-hand reminiscences and the trouble he took to delve into his past and to answer my questions.

For the second part of the book I am most grateful to John Gere who went through the manuscript and provided many helpful criticisms and improvements, in addition to translating the Latin epitaph on page 153. I should also like to thank Mrs Geoffrey Madan, who allowed me to borrow and to quote from A. C. Benson's letters to her husband, and Kenneth Rose who lent me E. F. Benson's Marlborough and Cambridge diary.

I am grateful to the Bodleian Library for allowing me access to the Benson Deposit; to the Wren Library for letting me inspect Archbishop Benson's diaries; to the Fawcett Library for allowing me to see the Strachey papers in their possession and to reproduce photographs of the Strachey children; and to the invaluable London Library.

FOREWORD

A favourite situation in Victorian novels was one where a solitary child, such as Florence Dombey in *Dombey & Son* or Sara Crewe in *A Little Princess*, stared across the street at the house opposite, where a rosy, happy group of boys and girls enjoyed the delights of belonging to a Large Family. The poor recluse watched them greeting Papa as he returned from the office, being read to by Mama after tea, going out for walks with Nanny and the New Baby, and his or her little heart was filled with envy. It is perhaps in something of the same spirit that we, children of the twentieth century, read about the families of Victorian days. In the upper and professional classes nowadays the average family is two or three. Many of us are only children. What was it like, we wonder, to form part of one of those bustling conglomerations?

There is no sense in generalisations. Each family then as now had its own particular ethos, made its own rules, was happy or unhappy in its own way. Yet because as a way of life the large family has almost vanished, I have thought it interesting to take two specimens of the genus and, without attempting to prove any particular point, to try to show, by means of their own writings, their diaries and their letters, most of which have not hitherto been published, how they behaved, what they felt and what they were like.

The two families, into whose lives I am endeavouring to peer, across the dividing street of Time, were almost exactly contemporaneous. Both sets of parents were married in 1859 and in each case the eldest child arrived punctually in the following year. The families had other things in common. Both formed part of the upper middle class stratum of English society; in particular they supported those two pillars of the Victorian age, the Indian Empire and the Established Church. Both were closely connected with Cambridge University; both were intellectually above the average and all the Bensons and most of the Stracheys wrote and published. It seems strange in view of these facts that the two families never seem to have met. The only time that the briefest contact was made was, as far as I am aware, on February 18th, 1918, when A. C. Benson read a paper on John Addington Symonds to a Cambridge dining-club. "Bertrand Russell was there," he records, "and a strange bearded creature who turned out to be Lytton Strachey."

This says much about the divisive structure of English class society. As far as family went, the Stracheys and the Grants were infinitely better placed than the Bensons and the Sidgwicks. The Stracheys were landed gentry in the reign of Queen Elizabeth and the Grants were descended from the Royal house of Scotland, but the Bensons, although with some trouble they managed to trace their forbears back to the fourteenth century, discovered, as Father Martindale, R. H. Benson's biographer, delicately puts it, that "the earlier estate of their ancestors [was] too undistinguished to promote enthusiasm." However, the enormous personal kudos appertaining to the higher branches of the Church hierarchy ensured that the Bensons moved into royal and aristocratic circles while the Stracheys remained in the professional upper class; a distinction that was very much more marked in Victorian times than most people imagine.

Another great dividing factor was that the Bensons'
own circle, not the one into which Canterbury had
thrust them, was, of course, the Church. The Archbishop's great achievement was the Lincoln Judge-
ment: a final adjudication on the thorny questions of
surplices and lights on altars. The Stracheys, on the
other hand, moved in the new world of the Darwins
and the Huxleys, of science and agnosticism, the apes
versus the angels.

Yet, though they never met, one strong characteristic marked both sets of parents; this was the certainty
and enormous self-confidence of the mid-Victorian age.
It was not a personal attribute. The Archbishop, the
most dominating of the four, suffered from neurasthenia and was often doubtful of his own individual
role. On one occasion, when Mr Gladstone had thrown
them over for dinner, Mrs Benson wrote that: "Your
father at breakfast said it was entirely due to a con-
tempt for him as the Archbishop." But in spite of such
occasional private uncertainties all the parents were,
in general, serenely confident about their age, their
country, their role in society and the continuance of
the same. They shared an unquestioning faith in
progress, in the future, and the betterment of the
human condition. By the end of the century, however,
this confidence was beginning to crack; they could not
transmit it to their children. It was a subtler, but
perhaps a larger, generation gap than the one we talk
so much of today, and its existence was demonstrated
in the simplest of all ways. The Stracheys had thirteen
children, ten of whom lived to maturity. The Bensons
had only six, but had it not been for Mrs Benson's
health (her first five babies arrived in seven years and

she was very ill after her last two confinements) they might well have rivalled the Stracheys. What happened in the next generation? The Stracheys had twelve grandchildren and the Bensons had none. The age of confidence and the day of the large Victorian family was over.

THE STRACHEYS

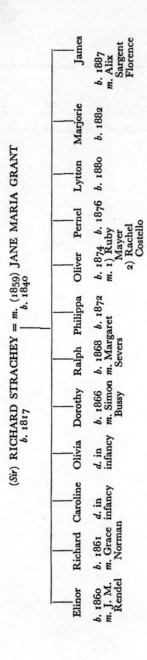

(*Sir*) RICHARD STRACHEY = *m.* (1859) JANE MARIA GRANT
b. 1817   *b.* 1840

Elinor	Richard	Caroline	Olivia	Dorothy	Ralph	Philippa	Oliver	Pernel	Lytton	Marjorie	James
b. 1860	*b.* 1861	*d.* in	*d.* in	*b.* 1866	*b.* 1868	*b.* 1872	*b.* 1874	*b.* 1876	*b.* 1880	*b.* 1882	*b.* 1887
m. J. M.	*m.* Grace	infancy	infancy	*m.* Simon	*m.* Margaret		*m.* 1) Ruby				*m.* Alix
Rendel	Norman			Bussy	Severs		Mayer				Sargent
							2) Rachel				Florence
							Costello				

Note. There was also another child, a boy, who died in infancy o 𝕀 o

"Lancaster Gate . . . is a . . . monumentally planned composition of tall well-to-do houses," writes
Nikolaus Pevsner in his *Buildings of England*. Monumental is the appropriate word. The tall, cliff-like
buildings, seven storeys high not counting the base-
ments, are indeed a monument to the wealthy middle-
class life of the mid-nineteenth century. In one of the
rear blocks of this gigantic development, effectively
cut off from any glimpse of a tree, stands No. 69, from
1884 to 1908 the home of the Strachey family.

In essence this Victorian terrace, where each house
once sheltered a single family, still subsists. The shallow flights of steps still rise between the pillared por-
ticoes the lancet windows still display their small
leaded panes, their tinted glass and, in the upper
lights, their conventional bouquets of flowers. The
"typical Bayswater stucco" as Pevsner calls it, is probably covered with the same grimy, cream paint,
within a shade or two, that it has worn for over a
century. Yet there are radical changes. Most of the
doorways are chained up, with a placard bearing the
words 'Fire Exit' attached to the chains. Only the door
of No. 73 remains open; a Stars and Stripes flag floats
above it and through its portals one can see neon
signs winking: Cocktail Bar, Powder Room, Television Lounge, for it is now an American Forces Club.
If one ventures within one finds that the interiors of
the six houses have suffered a devastating change.
Futuristic linoleum on the floors, a multitude of new
'toilets', a colour television, and everywhere American

17

soldiers, enormously fat sergeants, or wistful-looking Negroes, or very young boys with crew-cut hair. One passes through what had once been the drawing-rooms of six houses now all thrown into one gigantic cafeteria, containing a multitude of little tables, till at last one reaches the staircase that belongs to No. 69 and from here one can try to reconstruct the house as it was when the Stracheys occupied it from 1884 to 1908. The staircase itself, with its wrought-iron balusters and mahogany handrail, is probably unchanged and there is the great rounded skylight rising up in the centre of the house above the second floor, which Lytton Strachey described as being "a dome of pink and white glass". On the half-landing between the drawing-room and best bedroom floors there is still a bathroom which was once the only one in the house. There was no lavatory on the ground floor, the flushing of the plug was frequently heard in the drawing-room below. Above this domestic convenience and just under the dome, the staircase branches out onto a landing then vanishes. Research discovers a tiny flight which goes on and must continue almost indefinitely. Somewhere in those aerial heights was the nursery where Lytton, Marjorie and James spent their early years. Marjorie once wrote: "When we lived at Lancaster Gate Mama used to wear a little gold bell on her watch chain. The nursery was right at the top of a very high house, and the inhabitants were apt to feel lonely and cut off from the rest of the world. Suddenly one would hear the tinkling of the gold bell coming nearer and nearer. I shall never forget the exciting anticipation of interest and pleasure that came with it."

The isolation of the nursery and the immensely steep narrow stairs, which must have been exceedingly tiring to small legs, were not the only architectural drawbacks to Lancaster Gate. The whole house was singularly ill-proportioned and badly designed. There was no courtyard, no garden, the back windows were mostly of ground glass, and so little light came in that Lady Strachey had reflectors, huge plates of corrugated shiny material, hung on chains outside them. Some of the ground glass still subsists in back staircases and cubby-holes and it is so thick that one cannot see anything through it and on a grey winter's day almost no light filters through.*

The dark, narrow hall was, in the Stracheys' time, paved with a tessellated floor of magenta and indigo tiles. By the foot of the stairs were generally grouped two bicycles, incompletely covered with a rug and, in an alcove lined with red velvet thick with dust, stood a bust of the Venus de Milo. The dining-room was on the left of the hall. There took place those extraordinary Strachey meals which so amazed many visitors. They were served with some formality; the butler and the liveried boot-boy plodded round the table and three bottles of port, sherry and claret stood at one end and were ritually offered. (The wine, Lytton states, came from the grocer's round the corner.) The Stracheys almost never sat down less than eight and sometimes as many as twenty. When they were alone they read their books. When there was company there

---

* Since the above was written the Americans have vanished and at time of going to press the six houses are undergoing a massive reconstruction. Such traces as remained of the interior the Stracheys knew will be obliterated.

was, of course, conversation* and when "six or seven Stracheys became involved in an argument over the dinner-table, as almost always happened, the roar and rumble, the shrill shrieks, the bursts of laughter, the sound and fury of excitement was deafening and to an unprepared stranger paralysing".

Behind the dining-room was a narrow slip of space known as the 'young ladies room', described by Lytton as "a tiny apartment far higher than it was either long or broad, with a gigantic mahogany door, and the vast window, pink and frosted, with its string and ventilator, and a dim vision of filthy yellow bricks, chains and corrugations". Lady Strachey had no sitting-room of her own but was forced to keep her desk, overflowing with papers, in the dining-room. Sir Richard had a study on the half-landing, and there was an amorphous apartment on the ground floor, not much used, known as either the library or the schoolroom. All these rooms, with the exception of the dining-room, must have been plunged in Cimmerian twilight. A narrow stone staircase led to the basement where the servants existed in an even deeper gloom.

The Strachey servants almost deserve a chapter to themselves. Lady Strachey was a kind and considerate mistress. The little gold bell of which Marjorie wrote was inherited by a friend of the family who supposes

* Though not always. Virginia Woolf remembers her first luncheon party at Lancaster Gate where "innumerable Stracheys were seated in silence round the dinner-table. Pippa, who was presumably carving, broke the silence to ask: 'What will you have Papa? Cold beef or roast partridge?' 'Partridge,' said Sir Richard. Lady Strachey threw up her hands. 'I *knew* he'd say that!' she exclaimed. 'So *I* must have cold beef!' That was the only thing that anybody said I think."

it was to give notice of Lady Strachey's movements, so that if a footman should be studying the betting odds instead of polishing the silver or the kitchen-maid reading *Peg's Paper* instead of washing up they should have due warning. It must be admitted, however, that no Strachey kitchen-maid can have had much time to do anything but keep up with her duties. "Your Papa and I are actually alone," Lady Strachey wrote to Pernel in October 1898, "Pippa being in Scotland and Dorothy at Charlwood. It feels very queer to have luncheon alone." There must have been enough washing up to make a young girl very tired when she toiled up from the basement kitchen to a bed presumably situated on the top floor of the seven-storey house.

Lady Strachey, although she had great administrative talent, was an indifferent and unwilling housekeeper. "My ideal life would be to live entirely in *boarding-houses*," she once told Virginia Woolf, and indeed 69 Lancaster Gate must in some ways have greatly resembled one. She deputed the housekeeping duties to her daughters, first to Dorothy and after Dorothy's marriage to Pippa. At times the burden must have been heavy. "The Kingdon fiend,"* Pippa wrote to Pernel in April 1896 when her parents were in Biarritz, "evidently carried off pounds of *loaf* sugar and other stores in her boxes, and for a short time extreme excitement reigned in the lower regions, the kitchen-maid was given warning; Charlotte cooks more disgracefully than ever; the tradesmen's books are gross; *and* I have spent £136 since they left—one month. Isn't it fearsome? Gosling's has

* She refers to a defaulting cook.

written to complain and the world is nearly at an end."

In such circumstances the food, one must imagine, was bad and at times seems to have been insufficient.

"The Squire,"* wrote Dorothy in 1892, "is in excellent form and in a very good temper. There have been scarcely any public fracas except on one occasion at lunch when an omelette did not go round and he had to do without."

In 1900 Lady Strachey herself wrote gaily to Pippa describing the "painful scene" when an unexpected guest dropped in to luncheon. Sir Richard was in bed and a wing had already been served from the chicken for his benefit. "With great contriving Dorothy helped us all" (there were four of them) "and reduced the chicken to an absolute skeleton when a message was brought down that your Papa wanted some more!"

It was Marjorie who was the housekeeper when Lady Strachey took James and Duncan Grant out from St Paul's. She and the two hungry schoolboys returned anticipating "a delicious supper" and found nothing but a plate of biscuits and a bottle of soda water.

The buoyant and resilient temperament of the mistress of the house, however, rode as easily over such minor disappointments as it did over domestic difficulties.

Lytton Strachey describes the various butlers who served at different times. Frederick, the promoted gardener's boy, "uncouth, simian, with a great mouth, ill covered by a straggling moustache". "*Why* do the the Stracheys allow their man to have a moustache?"

---

* The Squire was Mr Elton, the husband of Sir Richard's first cousin, Minnie. He was presumably a guest in the house.

Marjorie overheard one military guest say to another as they left after one of Lady Strachey's at homes. "Bastiani a fat, black-haired, Italianate creature who eventually took to drink, could hardly puff up the stairs from the basement, and, as he handed the vegetables, exuded an odour of sweat and whiskey into one's face." Bastiani was succeeded by "Mr Brooks, who, we could only suppose, must have been a groom in earlier life, since all his operations were accompanied by a curious sound of *sotto voce* hissing". It is not altogether surprising to find Lady Strachey complaining mildly in 1901 that "the domestic crisis is still in full blast. The new boy and the new man have both given warning; the man arrived on Saturday night and gave warning on Sunday morning saying the work was too hard for him, and so said the boy. It is strange considering that there has never been a murmur about the work before, when the house has been twice as full."

Nor was the house-maiding in any way superior to the catering department at Lancaster Gate. The children scampering up and down the staircases and passages used to discover what they gleefully termed 'filth packets', behind furniture, in drawers and cupboards and in various odd corners. One can imagine those collections of swirls of grey dust, broken buttons, leadless pencils and rusty, forgotten keys.

Among all this dirt and discomfort the Strachey ladies were still waited upon, packed for and even had their hair done. This does not prove that they were unintelligent, lazy or helpless; it was simply the *mores* of their age and class. Lady Strachey wrote with amused bewilderment, when travelling with Sir

Richard, that the "great part of my occupation here is menial" (i.e. making afternoon tea and evening cocoa on the etna and washing up afterwards). "The rest of the time I spend over my hair (in which I continue to take a great interest)."

When she returned to London, however, she obviously found she had better things to do for in a letter to Pippa in 1908, during the upheaval that preceded the move to Belsize Gardens from Lancaster Gate, she wrote somewhat wistfully: "Don't you think that if she would agree it would be a good thing to keep on Ellen? We shall never get anyone to do our hair." Ellen, who was the most devoted of all the Strachey servants, seems to have originally entered the family as James' nurse. She became, however, in time a tower of strength to all the family. Continual letters contain messages asking Ellen to pack a red belt or to send on a blouse or to alter a skirt. As late as 1914 when Lytton was ill his mother wrote that he was "rather comforted by having Ellen to look after him".

She must have had a good deal of 'looking after' to do while she was with the Stracheys because, reading the family correspondence over the years, one is struck with the amount of illness that seems to have been prevalent at Lancaster Gate. The house resembled the Treacle Well in *Alice in Wonderland*, for any enquiry as to the inhabitants might at any time have been met with the rejoinder: "They were ill. Very ill." Basically Sir Richard and Lady Strachey must have been extraordinarily robust. He lived to 91 and she to 87 but minor complaints seemed to plague them and the whole family without ceasing. Influenza, measles, bilious attacks, sore throats and bad colds were continually afflicting them. This may have partly been due to the drains at Lancaster Gate. The great drain upheaval took place in 1896 when the Strachey parents were in Switzerland. The drains had obviously been under suspicion for some time because when Dorothy came down with a bad throat Lady Strachey wrote: "*Do* you think it is the drains? I cannot get your Papa to believe a word of it." It *was* the drains, which were described by Pippa as "foul, foulissimo", and the whole family had to decamp and be taken in by Elinor's in-laws. This wholesale operation, however, did not completely cure the family ills. Lady Strachey, returning from Paris in 1899, told Pernel that she found "your Papa rather unhappy and declaring his troubles had all come back. . . . Pippa is also very ill this morning with a bilious attack, Ball* has the commencement of a disease from which previously her life was despaired of, the under-housemaid has had fifteen teeth pulled out. . . . Dorothy is temporarily disabled by an unfortunately situated boil, and I am lame with rheumatism in the knee. Let us pass on."

And pass on she does; to the *Daily Telegraph* which she is sending Pernel; to news of Aunt Hennie and Aunt Lell; to her new book of nursery rhymes; to the second volume of Hugo's *Notre Dame* which Pernel is to get bound for Lytton; to her new dress which got sent to Paris by mistake and, finally, to Simon Bussy, an unknown French painter, a friend of Pernel's, one of whose pictures Sir Richard says he is willing to buy. He would, however, rather not pay for it till after Christmas and Lady Strachey adds, in her usual

* A housemaid?

25

warm-hearted way: "So as that may be inconvenient I will advance the money myself."

For the ugliness and the inconveniences of the material conditions at Lancaster Gate were amply balanced by a vivid, exciting and exacting social and intellectual life. The drawing-room running the whole width of the house was, according to Lytton Strachey, "its centre, its summary, the seat of its soul".

It was a large, badly proportioned room with three ogival windows looking out on the street and two fireplaces, one of which was a trophy of the Great Exhibition. It had been designed by Halsey Ricardo and Lytton wrote: "I cannot hope to describe that bulk of painted wood with its pilasters and cornices, its jars and niches, its marble and its multi-coloured tiles. . . . It combined, with an effect of emasculated richness, the inspiration of William Morris, reminiscences of the Renaissance, and a bizarre idiosyncrasy of its own."

Here every Sunday afternoon Lady Strachey was at home and here the enormous cohort of Strachey and Grant relations of all ages and of varying social levels and attainments ebbed to and fro. Here parties were given to which Lady Strachey asked so many people that "if they all come there will be a queue in the street—but"—she added hopefully—"they all won't come". Here there were musical soirées at which Joachim and Piatti played, and here, equally, the smaller fry of the family, James and Marjorie and their cousin Duncan Grant, who lived with them while his parents were in India, gathered round the piano and pounded out Gilbert and Sullivan, while Sir Richard and Lady Strachey sat benignly together at the far end of the room. Here Dorothy and Pippa twirled up and down in their white muslins with black sashes which they wore in 1888 as mourning for the German Emperor; here they gave evening parties; "Thursdays till Whitsuntide would be the best plan and I think small cards about the size of visiting cards ought to be printed"; and here they taught intellectual young men (including Leonard Woolf) how to dance Scotch reels.

Here Lady Strachey, Dorothy and Pippa paraded in their court dresses before "a select party of friends". Sheets were spread on the drawing-room floor and the trains were laid out at full length. Lady Strachey's dress was green satin with an embroidered front of pale pink and pearls and a black satin train brocaded with magnificent sprays of roses. The girls' dresses were, if we can believe their mother, whose dress sense seems to have been doubtful, "very pretty, Pippa all in white and Dorothy with a green and white train and pale pink embroidery over a white dress". The effect must have been somewhat spoilt by the inevitable Strachey pince-nez which were not discarded for the occasion. We learn from Pippa that Dorothy's pair, insecurely balanced, almost fell off onto the Queen's hand!

It was not only social occasions that the drawing-room witnessed. Here Lady Strachey used to read aloud to selected groups of girls Elizabethan dramatists (properly expurgated!) and poets. Lytton, a delicate eight-year-old boy, used to wander up and down the room listening and storing up in his capacious memory. Here too the children acted *John Gabriel Borkman*, the first time it was ever produced in England.

The spell of Lancaster Gate, of the crowded, dramatic, domestic life that went on behind this high ungainly front, is well described by Lytton. He writes of a recurring dream which frequently visited him. "For some reason or another—one of those preposterous and yet absolutely satisfying reasons which occur in dreams—we are back again, once more, just as we were, in Lancaster Gate. We are in the drawing-room among the old furniture, arranged in the old way, and it is understood that we are to go on there indefinitely, as if we had never left it. The strange thing is that, when I realise that this has come about, that our successive wanderings have been a mere interlude, that we are once more permanently established at number 69, a feeling of intimate satisfaction comes over me. I am positively delighted. And this is strange because, in my waking life, I have never for a moment, so far as I am aware, regretted our departure from that house, and if, in actuality, we *were* to return, I can imagine nothing which would disgust me more. . . ."

○ II ○

The Stracheys were an old English family; the Grants were an old Scottish clan; but the distinguishing characteristic that marked Richard Strachey and his wife was not their ancestral history in this island; but the fact that they were both Anglo-Indians.

Richard Strachey belonged to the golden period of British rule. One Indian historian puts it thus: "Centuries of toil on the part of the Moguls made no impression whatsoever on the task in hand, as they never enjoyed a sufficiently protracted period of peace to enable them to grapple with India's singularly difficult problems of domestic co-ordination. It was left to the ingenuity, industry and enterprise of the British to see the job through and within half a century very appreciable results were achieved."

After the selfish and unprincipled years of 'shaking the pagoda tree' there came a period when the English brought security and justice, pacified warring religions, built railways and founded universities.

Richard Strachey and his brother John were part of that almost legendary band of young men which included John Nicholson and the Lawrences who, under Mountstuart Elphinstone, served India with something of a religious dedication.

What was their motive? It was not for themselves it was not for the government at home; it was perhaps partly for India, for none of them escaped the fascination of that strange sub-continent; but it was mostly for the sake of the work itself. They held in their hands power and responsibility, they were stretched to the utmost, and their reward was the feeling that they were exercising their capacity to the full.

Kipling catches something of this spirit in his stories of bridge-builders and famine-relievers, and it is summed up by Lady Strachey in a letter written in 1897 addressed to her youngest son James, then aged ten years old:

"A very grand thing has happened to your Papa; he is to receive the Royal medal from the Royal Society. This is a very great scientific honour and it is given only to first rate men of science. . . . So you see what a number of classes your Papa is distinguished in; the military class, where he was mentioned in despatches and was given a brevet majority; the statesman class, where he received the prize of a grand star; and the scientific class where he has carried off a gold medal. But what I would like you particularly to know and remember is that these things are only *tokens* of good work; it is a pleasant thing, especially for a man's (or boy's) relations when these tokens prove that people know his work has been good, but the important thing is that a man should know it himself; and this is the fortunate case of many a one who never has letters after his name. Getting prizes of this kind is to a great extent accident; but without thinking of these, to do the best you can for the world you live in makes the difference between belonging to the Company of the great, whose lives have been a blessing to all mankind, to the little insect men who play about for an hour and perish."

It was this high-minded unquestioning principle that governed the lives of Richard and Jane Strachey; a calm certainty that was lost to their children.

Sir Richard Strachey seems to us, as he seemed to his children and their contemporaries, rather remote. This is not surprising as he was born three years before the accession of George IV. He was already a widower of 42 when in 1859 eighteen-year-old Jane Grant came into her father's drawing-room at Naini Tal and saw a small, black-haired man sitting on a yellow satin sofa. "Just the colours of a wasp," she commented unsentimentally. They were married a few months later and lived happily, if not ever after, at least till Sir Richard's death in 1908.

His energies seem to have been very little impaired by age. He retired from the Indian service to become chairman of the East Indian Railway in 1879, a post which he held for many years. He suffered a bad attack of dysentery in 1900 but early in 1901, when he was almost 84, Lady Strachey wrote to her son Ralph: "Your father is getting along pretty well except for his spirits. What really seems to do him good is a tough day at Nicholas Lane [the offices of the East India Railway]. Some question of an exciting nature has lately come home, and on Wednesday Sir Alex [Rendel] interviewed your father in bed about it. When he came downstairs he exclaimed, 'Don't tell me that man is ill—he has been most violent and headstrong, and is as stubborn as a bull—he *will* have his own way.' At 2½ your Papa drove down to the City, where he spent hours in arguing his point triumphantly, and did not get home till nearly 6. Here he found Mr Shaw and had an agreeable ½ hour's conversation on Meteorological matters [Sir Richard was chairman of the Meteorological Bureau and Mr W. N. Shaw its secretary] and was not only not a penny the worse but came down to dinner for the first time for a week."

It was not only in connection with public matters that Sir Richard gave proof of vital energy. He sired thirteen children after his late marriage and his youngest son was born when he was seventy.

This put him more in the place of a grandfather than a father to his younger children. The elder ones were much closer to him; indeed Philippa remembered that, as a child, they were more with him than with their mother, and it is perhaps worth noting that the elder members of the family were more conventional, more established and perhaps to a parent, more satisfactory than the younger siblings. It was when the household was more or less solely under the influence of the somewhat erratic and individual Lady Strachey that it became more unusual, more talented and more questioning. Sir Richard's growing, and finally almost total, deafness served to emphasise the separation between him and the daily life of Lancaster Gate. Visitors remember him as a small, snowy-haired old man, wrapped in a shawl, sitting at meals beside Lady Strachey in complete silence, or else comfortably installed in front of a blazing fire reading a novel, totally unaffected by the din of conversation and argument provided by his sons and daughters which raged around him. Nor was it only talk that he was able to ignore. "The reelers continue to reel," wrote Pippa to Lytton, "and we are beginning to take the weekly dance as a matter of course. We still

1. The Strachey Family. *Left to right:* Marjorie, Dorothy, Lytton, Pernel, Oliver, Dick, Ralph, Pippa, Elinor, James

2. The Strachey children:
1) Dorothy, 2) Pernel, 3) Pippa,
4) Lytton, 5) Ralph

make some faint efforts to shuffle it off and lengthen the interval but the enthusiasts with shining eyes settle the dates themselves! Papa serenely reads his novel throughout the performance."

Occasionally Sir Richard would be appealed to for his opinion and when he did take part in conversation the young found him both wise and delightful. Leonard Woolf remembers that: "he was extraordinarily friendly and charming to an awkward youth such as I was, and he was fascinating when now and again he was induced to enter the discussion or recall something from his past".

After the attack of dysentery previously referred to his life became more restricted and at ten o'clock at night the invaluable Ellen would appear to take him to bed. Duncan Grant wrote that he could "visualize distinctly Aunt Janie's expression" on these occasions. "As she sat playing patience on the opposite side of the elaborately tiled fireplace, she kept an agonized eye on Uncle Richard to see if he was going to be good or not. Sometimes he *was* good, soon closed his book rose with a smile, and shuffled off to bed on Ellen's arm. More often than not, as I seem to remember, he was naughty and resolved to finish his chapter before becoming aware that Ellen was in the room. Sometimes Ellen would bend forward and tell him it was late. No notice whatever was taken by Uncle Richard. Looks of sympathy were exchanged between Ellen and Aunt Janie, who shook her head in agonized disapproval. But as far as I remember she would never address a word herself to Uncle Richard, and if things became unusually drawn out, one of the young ladies would just put her book down and firmly advance and say, 'Papa dear, it's bedtime'. Realising that the game was up, Uncle Richard would raise his spectacles over his forehead and with an engaging smile pretend that this was the first time he had heard of it."

Nevertheless in spite of his age and remoteness his family loved and revered him. Many of them kept the letters he wrote them, signed according to the convention of an earlier day,

"Your afft. father

Rd. Strachey."

and they certainly show no lack of interest or of grasp. There is one to Pernel who has just succeeded in getting into Cambridge. It begins:

28th Oct/95

"My dear Pernel,
Enclosed is the means of discharging your debt to Newnham. It is rather odd that they have no formal way of stating what the fees are or of saying who is the person authorised to receive them. However I suppose the emancipated woman is above business bondage."

There is something a little pathetic in another letter which the eighty-one year old veteran wrote to his youngest son, then aged ten and a half. "You know I suppose that he [James's brother Oliver] is to go to India. . . . He is to go to the Railway on which Ralph is employed but not as an Engineer. He will be in the *Traffic* department. This is the branch that looks after the running of the trains, making arrangements for carrying goods and passengers—managing all the

34

Stations and guards—taking the money that people pay for their tickets and for sending goods and parcels. The Locomotive people manage the Engines and the Drivers and often they have to make all the Carriages and Wagons also. The Engineers have to look after the Rails, the Bridges, the Tunnels, and all the buildings, Stations and Houses and Warehouses of all sorts. It is a very complicated business altogether."

One feels that the old man is groping; trying to make contact with the boy, to interest him in a vital part of his own life. One feels also that James was not very much interested. Unlike the older members of his family he will never go to India.

Another rather touching letter is one that her father wrote to Pippa when she was in India. He had been very ill and was still "horribly persecuted with the most vicious indigestion". He questions Pippa closely on what she thinks of the East India railway and recalls the scenes of his youth, advising her if possible to get into the interior "so as to see some of the higher forest which is not seen in its true nobility below 10,000 or 12,000. . . . You will miss the greens and rounded forms of Switzerland but you will see what real big mountains are, which you cannot find there."

It is an unintentional stroke of pathos, for Sir Richard was a stoic, that the next paragraph begins: "I have not been able to get out very much lately, and only in a close carriage."

This eight-page letter concludes by asking Pippa to let him know what money she needs, for though he abandoned nearly all the daily arrangements of life to Lady Strachey Sir Richard always seems to have kept his control of the purse-strings; moreover he was very generous, perhaps especially to his daughters. Here he urges Pippa not to hesitate to get what is necessary to provide herself with a pony and not to be a burden on her brothers. "All this will require cash," he concludes, "and you must ask for it when it is wanted. I do not encourage you to play Baccarat, but make use of your life within the limit of reason."

It was a good summing-up from a man who had just passed his eighty-third birthday.

Jane Maria Strachey was at once a less distinguished and more unusual character than her husband. "It was my mother who counted," Dorothy Strachey once told a friend. "We got much more from my mother's family, the Grants, than from the Stracheys."

Jane Strachey's background was as Anglo-Indian as her husband's. Her grandfather had been sent out to India as a judge, in the old eighteenth-century days of political patronage, because he was unable to pay his debts at home, but her father Sir John Peter Grant was one of the great figures of the Indian administration, becoming in turn Governor-General of the Central Provinces and Lieutenant-Governor of Bengal.

After her marriage to Richard Strachey Jane, still in her twenties, became even more closely connected with the Government of India. During the sixties Richard's younger brother John Strachey was Judicial Commissioner to the Central Provinces and Richard himself was secretary to the Commission. They worked very closely together, discussing everything, and at these discussions "it was my pride and delight," Jane wrote, "to be present. Every paper written by my husband was brought to me to read over before it was finally dealt with, and verbal criticisms were freely allowed, and generally adopted." On one occasion Jane thought that a certain message might be more forcibly expressed and wrote out her suggested emendation. Her husband read it over and then remarked, as she says, "in a tone of deep disgust: 'What a clever old beast you are!' "

Such administrative duties by no means exhausted Jane Strachey's energies during her Indian period. She took part in all the gaieties of Simla, the croquet parties, the amateur theatricals and the dances. At the Bachelors' Ball the band played the final waltz so fast that her partner said: "This is an impossible pace; *we* can only just do it in time, and there is not anyone else in the room, at any rate, no other lady, who could." (Twenty-three years later at her daughter Dorothy's dance she records that she "took a turn . . . for old times' sake. I could show some of them the way yet!")

Such activities were punctuated by an almost incessant production of babies (there were seven born during the Indian period), and the consequent necessary shuttling to and fro between England and India, till in 1872, they came home for good.

Perhaps nothing in her future satisfied Jane Strachey more completely than her early married life in India. Dorothy Strachey wrote of her mother in *Olivia* . . . "Her chief passion in life was public affairs, Allied by birth and marriage to the aristocracy of Anglo-Indian families, the daughter and wife of great administrators, a profound interest in the craft of statesmanship was inherited in her blood and fostered by all the circumstances of her life." As Kipling wrote in *Plain Tales from the Hills* in a story where Mrs Hauksbee comes across a batch of Government papers not meant for her eyes: " . . . the first glimpse of the naked machinery of the Great Indian Government, stripped of its casings, and lacquer, and paint, and guard-rails, impresses even the most stupid man. And Mrs Hauksbee was a clever woman. She was a little afraid at first and felt as if she had taken hold of a lightning-flash by the tail." It was this naked machinery that Jane Strachey saw and understood and even influenced during her Indian years; she would never again be so close to the levers of power. Nevertheless her life in England was to be a very full one and the ensuing twenty years was headed "Golden Days" in her autobiography.

The Stracheys settled first of all in a house on the edge of Clapham Common, where five more children were born. Perhaps this house, which they had called Stowey House after the family seat, became too small, for in 1884 they took the enormous 69 Lancaster Gate where they remained for the next twenty-four years. It was during this period that the Stracheys as a collective family unit reached their zenith, guided, controlled and shaped by the nerve-centre of the household: Mama.

Jane Strachey was a tall, somewhat ungainly woman with unusually long arms, dressed in bunchy, un-fashionable clothes, very often of black satin, with Venetian lace on the bodice. She was short-sighted and exceedingly absent-minded. "She would walk into the room in a kind of dreamlike way", wrote Leonard Woolf, "gaze uncertainly about her and then

walk out again." He imagined that she had come to
fetch something she had forgotten and had then forgotten what that something was.

In spite, however, of her lack of grace and of mus-
cular co-ordination (she was so accident-prone that
her autobiography contains a chapter entitled simply
"Accidents"), Lady Strachey suffered from no lack
of self-confidence. When her husband received the
G.C.S.I. she complained that she would now become
one of the many Lady Stracheys instead of being
"*the* Mrs. Richard Strachey". She overflowed with
superabundant vitality and what strikes one, as one
reads over her diaries, recollections and letters, is the
astonishing amount she managed to put into her life,
the immense energy she displayed and the calm and
imperturbable good humour with which she met
every rub and difficulty. Her letters alone are a
marvel. To every child, and there were ten of them,
she seems, if she or they were away from home, to
have written on an average about once a week. The
letters to her three sons in India have not been pre-
served but I feel sure that she wrote by every mail;
and to Dorothy in the South of France, to Pippa in
Scotland, to Pernel at Newnham, to Lytton at Liverpool, to Marjorie at Allenswood, to James at Rugby,
the letters flowed out regularly. It is not a very
amusing correspondence, nor is it of a high literary
quality; Lady Strachey's letters give family gossip and
plans, comment on the recipient's news, occasionally
deal with public events. There is an unusual touch of
descriptive power when she describes Queen Victoria's
funeral procession: "the guarded road like a wide
ribbon, and beyond the mass of black, the whole

depth of the park, topped with a wash of pink which was the faces". But, on the whole, the letters are a domestic chronicle dealing with illnesses, servants and news about brothers, sisters and relations. They are, in fact, just what a lonely child at school or a son in far-off India would like to have. They breathe an atmosphere of stability, security and love. They are all written in the same small, legible, almost copper-plate handwriting and they invariably end "Ever your loving Mama". No more appropriate signature could be imagined.

If any child were ill or in trouble he or she could count on Mama. Reading a Life of Lytton Strachey one might imagine that his mother's whole energies were taken up with taking him to the doctors, to the seaside, to arranging foreign travel for him. He was certainly the most delicate and perhaps the most anxiously cared for of her children, but reading the broader spectrum of her letters one finds her sleeping on a sofa during Elinor's confinement and feeding her every two hours, travelling to Yorkshire to nurse Pernel who had caught diphtheria on a reading party or popping down to Rugby to comfort a very homesick little James in his first term, "but you must promise not to cry when I go away again".

Nor was she a possessive or jealous mother, She welcomed her children's friends; she found it natural that Lytton should prefer his sisters' company to hers. She had her own life and her own preoccupations. People, of course, were in the forefront. 'Papa' occupied the greatest space, then there was 'Aunt Lell', her dearly beloved sister Elinor, Uncle Trevor, who was also beloved but much more of a problem,

Aunt Hennie who was slightly deficient, and number-less other aunts, uncles and cousins. We find her in-volved in letting Uncle Trevor's flat, finding a home for Aunt Hennie and arranging art tuition for her nephew Duncan Grant.

Yet although in her care for her children she was the complete antithesis of Mrs Jellyby, she did have a very full and varied life of her own. She was much concerned for the Women's Movement and a great friend of Dame Millicent Fawcett's. She frequently spoke at public meetings, and she wrote "An Inter-national Song" dedicated to the International Alli-ance of Women's Suffrage Societies. The chorus goes:

> *Nearer still and nearer*
> *To our glorious goal*
> *March we on together*
> *With undaunted soul.*
> *North and South are banded*
> *East and West as one*
> *Hail the Dawn of Freedom*
> *The rising of the Sun.*

It was set to music by her brother, Bartle Grant, and the music reaches about the same standard as the words.

It must be admitted that her output as an author was not remarkable. She wrote a play for children called *Little Boy Blue*, some verses entitled *Nursery Lyrics* and the words of some songs for "singing-class music".

She also edited the diary of her aunt, Elizabeth Grant of Rothiemurchus, under the title of *Memories of a Highland Lady*, which gives a very fascinating picture of the manners and customs of the late eighteenth century. In addition she wrote her own autobiography, *Some Recollections of a Long Life*, part of which was published in the *Nation and Athenaeum*.

Yet, although her creative talents were strictly limited, she possessed a great knowledge of and devotion to both French and English literature. Leonard Woolf describes her as "passionately intellectual". She had studied the French Encyclopaedists and the Elizabethan dramatists. She knew much of Milton by heart and on her first voyage to America she learnt the whole of Gray's *Progress of Poesy*, and used to get up at 6.30 to walk round the deck and repeat the lines for the day. She adored Jane Austen, quotations from whose works frequently figure in her letters. She was a great personal friend of George Eliot's, whom she deeply revered. She would have made a remarkable and inspiring teacher. Even as it was, she did not keep her erudition and enthusiasm to herself. Naturally she read aloud to her own children, "[I] am now in the middle for the how many-eth time—of *Pride and Prejudice*", and she also gave readings of the Elizabethans to small classes of girls from her daughters' school, Allenswood, and more general poetry readings at Leighton House. Leonard Woolf recalled that she read poetry superbly and would often read aloud to himself and Lytton. "I have never known anyone live so completely in the poetry or play or prose which she read aloud or recited." He describes an occasion when he saw her not long before she died in 1927. It was a summer evening in the garden of Gordon Square. "Virginia and I sat under the weeping ash tree there and talked with her. She was blind, rather feeble, and old now, but seemed to me in-

domitable. We talked about books and poetry and
'Lycidas', and she recited 'Lycidas' straight through
from end to end. And it was just the same as it had
been twenty-five years before; it was superb; you felt
for five minutes that the world she was in was the world
of Milton and 'Lycidas'."

She had, of course, her limitations. "With all her
love of literature, music and painting," Dorothy
Strachey wrote, "with all her vivid intelligence my
mother, I think, never felt them otherwise than with
her mind. She was perhaps incapable of the mystical
illumination. To speak on a lower plane, she surround-
ded herself with ugly objects; her furniture, her pictures, her clothes were chosen not without care but
without taste" (when one remembers Lady Strachey's
outfit for the drawing-room one can only silently
assent); "she was incapable of distinguishing food or
wine." Although, Dorothy concludes, her home was
"very rich in intellectual influences of many sorts,
there was in it a curious, an almost anomalous
lack—an insufficient sense that is—of humanity and
art".

From all we have seen of Lancaster Gate we can
agree that the second is fairly obvious. Art and taste
were both lacking—but humanity? Perhaps the ab-
stract noun is wrongly chosen and that what Dorothy
meant was sensuality, using the word in no pejorative
sense. Together with beauty it is possible that
Lancaster Gate lacked understanding warmth. Dorothy
says that her mother was "strangely devoid of psychology and strangely unconscious of persons. She
never had a notion of what any of us children were
doing or thinking, and intrigues of the most obvious

and violent nature might be, and indeed often were, carried on under her nose."

Dorothy, Lytton and Marjorie, possibly the three most sensual members of Lady Strachey's family, suffered most from this lack of temperament; and there is, if one wishes to be unkind, a sort of chirping complacency about Lady Strachey's letters, diaries and reminiscences: an echo of Gilbert's lines, "For I am right and you are right and all is right as right can be," which must at times have been aggravating.

Yet in some ways it probably provided her children with an armour against the world. Lady Strachey, trained in the full consciousness of Victorian rectitude and Anglo-Indian supremacy, was convinced that she, her husband and her family were splendid, remarkable and right; and some of this rubbed off onto her children. There is no doubt that they all felt that to be a Strachey was to rejoice in the "tranquil consciousness of effortless superiority", even though they questioned and, in most cases, rejected her basic values, her beliefs and her certainties.

Lady Strachey herself must have had a hard time keeping up with her children. The first major blow came in 1903 when Dorothy became engaged to a penniless French painter, of peasant origin, Simon Bussy. 'Little Bussy,' as they called him, had been helped, patronized and encouraged by the family but Lady Strachey certainly never envisaged him as a possible husband for one of her daughters. "Lancaster Gate," wrote Lytton, "was shaken to its foundations," but there was no break and no unkindness.

A much greater blow at a later date must have been Lady Strachey's two younger sons becoming

'conchies' in the First World War. As we have seen
although she considered herself advanced and was,
for instance, a staunch agnostic,* Lady Strachey in
most ways was a true mid-Victorian. Above all, she
held the simple, patriotic convictions of her time and
—I was going to write 'and class'—but actually the
enthusiasm for Queen and Empire was not confined
to the upper and middle classes. "Pippa and Elinor
both take weekly money to some Reservist families,"
Lady Strachey wrote during the Boer War. "They all
repudiate with horror any idea of giving in; one of
them said the soldiers would not hear [of] it; 'You
see Miss, what *they* think on is the country.' " This was
exactly Lady Strachey's own attitude. When Virginia
Woolf during the 1914-1918 war asked her if she liked
any modern poetry, "she shook her head in a melancholy way and pursed her lips. Then suddenly her
face lit up. 'Yes! We've one living poet—one great
living poet!' she exclaimed—'Admiral Hopwood!' He
had written a patriotic poem which she had cut out
of the *Times* and read to us."

Yet she never criticised Lytton and James for
evading war service any more than she criticised them
for sexual *mores* which must have been antipathetic
to her. Did she know about them? We cannot be quite
certain, although Oliver† had been sent down from
Balliol for a slip in that direction of which she must

* Although even in this she showed a certain respect for
convention. She had all her children christened and she attended
church in the country although not in London.
† Once Oliver had escaped from the monastic system of
British upper-class education he became normally heterosexual,
married twice, and was, according to Michael Holroyd, "something of a womanizer".

have been cognizant. She may have deliberately shut her eyes; we have Dorothy's evidence that "she never had a notion of what any of us children were doing or thinking," but was not that perhaps one of her great strengths as a mother? Who could have borne to have had a perceptive, psychologically understanding parent continually on the *qui vive*? "Oh how dreadful to be a mother. How terrible to love so much and know so little!" wrote Lytton. "Will it always be like this to the end of the world?" But it was the loving that was important. The Stracheys were blessed in that they knew whatever happened, whatever they did or failed to do, there would always be in the background an unfailing source of strength and reassurance, their "Ever loving Mama".

○ III ○

The Strachey family bore a great resemblance one to another. Bertrand Russell, describing his first visit to Lancaster Gate, wrote: "All the children were to my unpractised eyes exactly alike except in the somewhat superficial point that some were male and some were female. The family were not all assembled when I arrived, but dropped in one by one at intervals of twenty minutes. . . . I had to look round the room carefully to make sure that it was a new one that had appeared and not merely one of the previous ones that had changed his or her place. Towards the end of the evening I began to doubt my sanity, but kind friends afterwards assured me that things had been as they seemed."

The Stracheys themselves seem to have been aware of this family likeness. Pippa, writing to Lytton at school when he had the measles, said: "We are all truly sorry for you, you poor thing, and if we could do what we liked you would long ago have seen your door fly open and a swarm of creatures in spectacles and eyeglasses come hurrying in to console you."

It was, of course, their thin, rather spidery figures,* the ubiquitous spectacles and above all the family voice, light, high, at times almost rising to a squeak, and with unexpected stresses, that stamped the Stracheys. Pippa, in India, was accosted in the hotel at Bombay by a completely strange lady who asked if she

* Marjorie alone was massive, taking after her mother.

were "Miss Strachey". "Wasn't it weird? . . . She had not heard a word of my being in India or expected in India and had simply spotted me from the family likeness and been quite convinced by the voice."

It was, of course, the Strachey voice and intonations transmitted by Lytton that was to become one of the distinguishing features of 'Bloomsbury'.

Nevertheless, there were marked differences among the family, though these never seemed to have affected their family solidarity or their pleasure in each other's company.

Dick, the eldest son, was perhaps the least interesting of the brothers. He was in the Regular Army, commanded the Rifle Brigade and married his C.-in-C.'s daughter, Grace Norman. "I think she is very nice and the extreme talkativeness has worn off," was the rather sister-in-law-like comment made by Pippa to Pernel during the engagement. Possibly a somewhat invidious remark to come from one of the Stracheys!

Like many regular officers when the war actually came, Dick was rather too old for it (he was fifty-two in 1914), and was passed over for a job he thought he ought to have had. Although frequently at home during his leaves from India he appears to have made little impact on the rest of the family, though there is a pleasant scene recounted by Pippa when he and Oliver, with stirring cries of "Haro",* endeavoured to weigh his bicycle on the weighing machine which, in true Lancaster Gate fashion, seems to have stood inside the dining-room.

* "Haro" or "Ha rok" was the ancient Norman hue and cry and the exclamation made by those who wanted assistance, their person or property being in danger.

3a. Lady Strachey

3b. Sir Richard and his daughters. *Left to right:*
Elinor, Marjorie, Pernel, Dorothy, Pippa

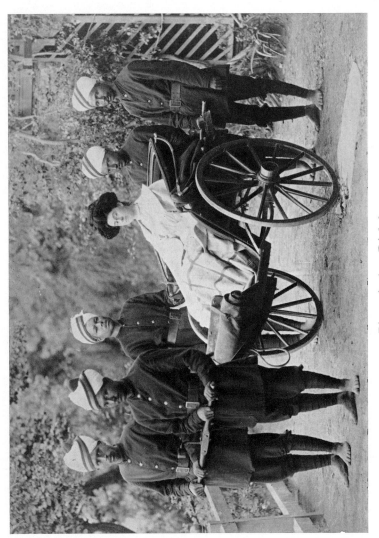

4. Pippa in her Rickshaw

Ralph, the next son, also spent most of his life in India; he was not in the Army but held a high-up post in the Engineering department of the East Indian Railway. He seems more incorporated with the rest of the family than Dick, partly because he was Pippa's favourite brother, and though his letters home are not as a rule very interesting he could occasionally sparkle, as is shown by a charming triolet which he wrote to Pernel when she came out top in her French exams. The first verse goes

> *Je suis si fier*
> *Je chante et danse*
> *Je suis le frère*
> *(Je suis si fier)*
> *De la jeune première*
> *En langue de France.*
> *Je suis si fier*
> *Je chante et danse.*

The Strachey clannishness and family feeling is shown by Oliver when he wrote about Ralph's future wife, Margaret Severs: "It would be difficult to select a female (outside the family) that would quite come up to one's standard for Ralph—He is *the* blessing of India to me—(when we meet we do nothing but giggle from morn till dewy eve)."

Margaret, alas, does not seem to have been a giggler and she was not greatly liked by her relations-in-law. "How like Margaret to arrive just so as to spoil your holiday!" Lady Strachey wrote to Pippa in 1914, adding in brackets "(a nice mother-in-lawish remark)".

Oliver, the third Strachey son, was also endeavouring to make his career in India but this was from necessity rather than choice. As has already been mentioned, he was sent down from Balliol, a homosexual letter having been found in his rooms, and was sent off for a tour round the world with Robert Bridges as a tutor. After that, at his own earnest request, he went to study music in Vienna. He was very gifted both musically and mathematically, the two, as they so often do, running concurrently, but it appeared obvious after a year in Austria that he had not got the skill or the creative ability to make music his career. So it had to be India. Lady Strachey wrote with unusual severity that: "I had a talk with him [Oliver] this morning, when he professed his willingness to do anything of any sort or kind and I tried to rub it into him that he had cut himself off from any chance of profitable employment. Your Papa then said he thinks he can get him something to do in India on the railway and I was glad to hear Oliver murmur that it was very good of him. It is a miserable business."

So Oliver went to India, in the Traffic Department, as Sir Richard had painstakingly explained to James, and worked hard, and became interested in freight rates and considerably enlivened Dinapore where he was stationed. But his heart was not in it. "The great pain of this place," he wrote to Pernel, "is that nobody in India has ever read a book, or looked at a picture, or ever thought, or even spoken to anybody who has ever thought about anything but horses." He, too, married in India, more rashly than Ralph, for his salary was very much less, and he seems to have been less enthusiastic about his bride. She was a German girl whose father was a contractor and maker of bricks. "As you don't know India I can hardly make you realise the snobbishness of it—but people who make bricks, and

Germans, are quite out of society," Oliver wrote to Pernel, and went on: "Pernie darling, *don't* take a dislike to her now for heaven's sake. She is really a good girl, and I'm very fond of her;—I should be *very* unhappy if the family did not get on with her—especially you." The family, on the whole, seem rather to have preferred Ruby to Margaret, although in the end it was Ruby who ceased to be a member of the Strachey clan, for after she and Oliver returned to England, she left him and their three-year-old daughter Julia—about whom she had written so many rapturous letters to her in-laws. But this is, as another Anglo-Indian put it, "another story".

So much has been written of Lytton Strachey that it hardly seems necessary to add to the volume. It may, however, be worth pointing out that at home, at any rate in early days, he seems to have been considered a light-hearted and lively boy and he certainly struck sparks from his sisters, particularly from Pippa. Her letters to "My dearest Folderol", as she sometimes styled him, are gayer and funnier than to any other of her family. Their eyes obviously frequently met in amusement. For instance, in 1895 when he was at school in Leamington, she wrote: "I have a great many entertaining anecdotes and I longed for you to share the jokes. The worst is that without you I am quite as preternaturally solemn as the most solemn Wimble-donite." (The reference is to Miss Souvestre's school at Wimbledon where Dorothy was teaching and Pernel and Marjorie were still being educated.)

Another letter seems to refer to a local clergyman: "Lytton Lytton To you I must direct my Wail! Alas je suis tombée dans l'amour. Headlong! And there is no hope for me for the place—the blessed place of help-meat [*sic*] to the Beloved is already occupied. Woe is me! Unworthy as I feel her to be of her high fortune the chains of custom are all too strong for me to hope to break them armed though I be with the powers given by *true* appreciation of him and complete forget-fulness of self in my devotion to his *best* interests . . . it was last night that my reluctant—my recalcitrant heart was captured. Space is lacking for even an out-line of his conversation but I need not tell you that not a word of it is forgotten, still less the enchanting eagerness with which he concealed behind the writing-paper box a brown pamphlet which he had brought with him for you 'a parochial address' as he termed it for parishioners *only* in spite of which warning I had torn it from its hiding place and was busy perusing it almost before his lanky form had vanished behind the portière. Vanished! Vanished!"

The high-spirited hyperbole of this nonsense is not dissimilar from Lytton's letters to his friends at Cam-bridge. When Duckworth broke his leg by falling off his bicycle Lytton wrote to Maynard Keynes that he wondered "how soon the news would spread abroad, and how many people his bedroom would be able to hold. These thoughts still agitate and blast me. I am consumed by terrors. We live upon a cataract; and at any moment, while we are yawning at the Decemviri, or maundering at McT's, the Hope of the World may be crushed to smithers by a cart in Trinity Street."

Lytton was doubtless more emotionally involved with Duckworth than Pippa was with the anony-mous caller. Nevertheless the style is the same.

How early his sisters knew about his homosexuality is not clear. Lady Strachey sent two of them out of the room when she argued with Lytton that Shakespeare could not possibly have been a homosexual, but they probably knew more than she did. As early as 1900 Oliver was writing to Pernel: "I got a strange letter from Lytton" (just gone to Cambridge) "from which I conceive him to be in the stage of most painful prigdom. . . . The letter was in 'phrases' so to speak with metaphors, climaxes, aposiopeses etc. all complete. *Most* extraordinary! Also relating of his study of 'the human youth'—This of course is highly confidential. . . ." At a later date when Pippa had nursed Lytton through one of his many illnesses, he said: "Do you think—we are so happy together—that we could live together?" It was an appeal and Pippa realised it, but though moved and miserable she could only remain speechless and after a long pause he said sadly: "No, you hate my habits—I can't do without them. It is no use." The subject was not referred to again; but Lytton always retained his deep affection for Pippa. She amused him as no-one else did; she was beside him when he died and, as he lay desperately ill with a temperature of 104°, her well-known screeching laugh was heard and brother and sister were dissolved in hopeless giggles over some family joke.

In time, of course, Lytton got tired of and rebelled against what he regarded as the smothering, feminine, mother-sister atmosphere of Lancaster Gate but he generally retreated under its wings when he felt ill and it was not till he found a nanny-sister-companion in Dora Carrington that he threw it off entirely. In earlier days he could hardly move a step without one of his family, and when, after the shattering experience of finding out that Duncan Grant had fallen in love with Edgar Duckworth, he caught 'flu in Paris, he had to send for Pippa to bring him home.

"My dear Pippa," he wrote, in a rather pathetic pencil scrawl, "I find that Duncan has sent off his letter to you asking you to come here. It would be the greatest comfort if you could, though I'm afraid the trouble involved is enormous. I have got a feverish cold, which seems to be on the road to influenza. I feel that it is rather appalling to make the wretched Duncan perform the functions of garde-malade, and I don't feel as if I could face the journey back by myself."

Lytton at this time was twenty-six.

Amateurs of psychoanalysis may perhaps pounce on the fact that Lady Strachey, like Lady Wilde, dressed her son in petticoats and left his hair long for the first years of his life—not because she wanted a daughter, she already had four—but because he looked prettier that way. A possibly more valid cause of his homosexuality was the undoubted fact that in early years he had a passionate devotion to his mother.

When he was read Macaulay's lines:

For how can man die better than facing fearful odds
For the ashes of his fathers and the temples of his gods

he was heard to murmur: "For their *mothers*".

If one is going to dabble at all in psychoanalysis it might be just worth noting that many of his troubles, his insecurity, his feeling that he was unloved, and his frequent ill health, some of which may have been a bid for love and attention, may partly date from the birth of his brother James.*

The arrival of Marjorie, two years younger than himself, seems for some reason to have posed no threat to his position as Lady Strachey's favourite child. When, however, James Beaumont came on the scene in 1887 it was rather different. 'Jembeau,' to give him his family nickname,† was something of an *enfant du miracle*, since his father was seventy and his mother forty-seven when he was born. His sister Elinor's children were older than he was and he was known in the nursery as "Uncle Baby".

Moreover, he was just the sort of little boy to appeal to Lady Strachey: gentle, intelligent and precocious. His letters from his prep. school much resemble those of other little boys—my place in form; we beat X by three goals to two; we had fish for dinner; there is nothing more to say; but suddenly one comes upon a postscript which reads, "I have just this moment heard of Faure's death" (Felix Faure, French President), "how shocking it will be for France. It seems she will collapse altogether." One can imagine how Lady Strachey would have welcomed this interest in public affairs.

She obviously adored him. Her letters are signed as to the rest of the family, "ever your loving mama", but they are sprinkled with endearments, "my darling love", "my loveling", "my darling bird".

* It is interesting to note that Lytton does not seem to have been born a delicate child. Pippa told Carrington that he had suffered from illness "ever since he was five years old". This was of course two years before James's birth, but after a lapse of forty years and in the course of general conversation it is possible that Pippa was not absolutely accurate as to date.

† He was known indifferently as Jimbeau or Jembeau, a contraction of James Beaumont.

"I have always thought Jembeau exceedingly like Cowper," she confided to Pernel, "so affectionate, gentle and timid in disposition, and trenchant in intellect." His sisters were not quite so uncritical. "Jimbeau is very bumptious. Mama says he is a very meek lamb trying to give himself the airs of a lion," wrote Pippa to Lytton, "but my private opinion is he is a fierce lion disguised as a lambkin." But they too spoiled him, wrote to him continually. There are letters in rhyme, letters purporting to come from his beloved cat Christopher and letters enclosing little coloured pictures, anything that might amuse and distract a cherished little boy for the first time away from home. His nurse Ellen wrote:

"My darling Jembeau

You have been away 5 days and not send [*sic*] me a card or letter to say how you are. I hope you are enjoying your dear little self and that you are well. I shall expect to see rosy cheeks tomorrow Thursday."

And Mlle Schaller, who had been with them since Clapham Common days and was perhaps caricatured out of all likeness by Lytton in *Ermyntrude and Esmerelda*, wrote pages on very thin paper, in that sloping spidery hand so characteristic of French governesses, assuring her "*petit coco chéri*" that "*il vit et vivra toujours dans mon cœur*".

In the fulness of time the balance shifted but it seems a possible theory that Lytton, who went to boarding school for the first time two years after the advent of this idolised little creature, may, in spite of the family affection which surrounded and buttressed him, have felt a longing to excel in some intellectual sphere and to be indisputably first with some creature in a perfect and fulfilled love.

○ IV ○

Elinor was the eldest and the prettiest of the Strachey
sisters. She was one of the only two to marry and the
only one to make what, in those days, would have been
regarded as a 'satisfactory' marriage. Her husband was
Jim Rendel, the son of Sir Richard's colleague on the
East India Railway, Sir Alexander Rendel. He was
a rising barrister and they lived in a large house
in Melbury Road and produced five children who
frequently came round to Lancaster Gate to play with
James. It was considered a great joke that their uncle
was younger than they were. "Please pardon me for
addressing you without the word 'Uncle'," wrote the
eleven-year-old Ellie to the nine-year-old James, "it
was a slip of the pen and no disrespect was meant."
She signed herself "your dutiful and affectionate niece".
  One would like to know more of Elinor. Marjorie
once said that she was the cleverest of the sisters. One
anecdote of her childhood is charming. It was at the
height of the Darwin controversy and the Stracheys,
as liberal, broadminded intellectuals, were naturally
strongly on Darwin's side. Elinor, taken to the zoo, saw
the monkeys playing in their cages, and immediately
exclaimed: "Little brothers, little cousins". "You can
imagine," recorded Lady Strachey, "how delighted
her father was." The brief reminiscences that Elinor
jotted down on her mother's death show that she
shared the family talent for the written word. "She was
immensely courageous," wrote Elinor, "and, perhaps

57

her most endearing quality, a fountain of never failing enthusiasm. How she loved, and made you love, her many favourites! Her Elizabethans, the Cause of Women, John Stuart Mill, Scott, the French Revolution, Mazzini, Robert Browning, George Eliot, Mario —all these were stamped indelibly on my youthful mind.

"She had a very special love for France. When I was about fifteen she took me to Mlle Souvestre's school at Fontainebleau and I remember how, as the train approached Paris and we were entering its dingy, grey suburbs, Mama rose to her feet in the carriage, drew herself up and saluted the great city. I never forgot it." What an excellent picture this gives of Lady Strachey!

As a boy Oliver Strachey wrote a poem to his mother and father which concluded with the following verse:

> *Five sons and five daughters are their's*
> *Who—strange to say, all go in pairs;*
> *The eldest's a wife,*
> *And the youngest's seen life*
> *For one year in the nursery upstairs.*

The second line of the jingle is almost, though not quite, accurate. The family did divide into pairs. Elinor and Dick in early days; Ralph and Pippa; Pernel and Oliver; and, in their childhood, Lytton and Marjorie. This left over James, the general pet and plaything, and Dorothy.

Two little girls had been born and died between Dick and Dorothy, one of them named Olivia, and it was perhaps the memory of a fantasy desire for a close companion that led Dorothy to name her book after her little dead sister. She seems to have been a shade lonely in that close-knit family circle and when she followed Elinor to Mlle Souvestre's school she found there, as those who have read *Olivia* will remember, an emotional consolation that was almost too rich and perturbing.

Marie Souvestre, the Mlle Julie of *Olivia*, was the daughter of a now forgotten but once eminent French author. She started a girls' school when she was quite young, a daring thing to do in those days, in partnership with a Mlle Dussaut. They were obliged to quit France during the German occupation of 1870 and they went to Florence with the few girls left under their care. There Marie Souvestre met Lady Strachey. "She fell in love with me at once," wrote the latter in perfect innocence.

What shades of emotion on Mlle Souvestre's side are contained in this statement we cannot tell. The chance encounter certainly led to an enduring and deeply rooted friendship. But more than friendship was in question when Dorothy Strachey followed Elinor to the Fontainebleau school, Les Ruches, in 1882.

It is impossible to say how far *Olivia* is strictly auto-biographical. Undoubtedly the emotion recollected in tranquillity with which the book is written must have had its basis in fact. "Love has always been the chief business of my life." states the introduction, "the only thing I have thought—no, felt—supremely worth while and I don't pretend that this experience was not succeeded by others. But at that time, I was innocent, with the innocence of ignorance. I didn't know what was happening to me. I didn't know what was happening to anybody. . . . How should I have known indeed, what was the matter with me? There was no

instruction anywhere. The poets it is true . . . had a way
of talking sometimes which seemed strangely to illum-
luminate the situation. But this, I thought, must be an
illusion or an accident. What could these grown-up
men and women with their mutual love-affairs have in
common with a little girl like me? My case was so
different, so unheard of. Really no one had ever heard
of such a thing, except as a joke. Yes, people used to
make joking allusions to 'schoolgirl crushes'. But I
knew well enough my crush was not a joke. And yet I
had an uneasy feeling that, if not a joke, it was something to be ashamed of, something to hide desperately.
This I suppose was not so much a matter of reflection
(I did not think my passion was reprehensible, I was
far too ignorant for that) as of instinct."

It is obvious that this first encounter with what she
calls the 'sensual element' hitherto lacking in her life,
had a profound influence on Dorothy Strachey—not
only on the romantic but on the intellectual side. Mlle
Souvestre's keen intelligence, her appreciation of literature, her superb reading of Racine, Lamartine and de
Vigny, kindled in the young girl a flame of devotion to
French literature, to the whole spirit of France, which
were to colour her life. How far the schoolgirl adora-
tion was reciprocated, how much of *Olivia* was truth,
how much artistry, how much wish fulfilment, we shall
never know. Certainly Dorothy's mother suspected
nothing; certainly the emotion must have died down
and been dispersed. It was more artistic that the object
of devotion should die, far away in Canada, leaving her
adorer an ivory paper knife "with her name engraved
on it: JULIE", but in actual fact, after disassociating
herself from her partner (there seems to have been a

quarrel, but no death nor any suspicion of murder)
Mlle Souvestre went not to Canada but, less pictur-
esquely, to Wimbledon, where she started another
school called Allenswood, where Pernel and Marjorie
were both educated (without as far as we know any
emotional complications) and where Dorothy was to
go as an auxiliary teacher. Life resumed its even,
everyday flow with a hidden memory perhaps of some
deeply emotional moments that were never to be
forgotten. "It was to me she was reading. I knew it.
Yes, I understood, but no one else did. Once more that
sense of profound intimacy, that communion beyond
the power of words or caresses to bestow, gathered me
to her heart. I was with her, beside her, for ever close
to her, in that infinitely lovely, infinitely distant star,
which shed its mingled rays of sorrow, affection and
renouncement on the dark cold world below."

We have few clues to Dorothy's love life between
Mlle Souvestre and the advent of Simon Bussy, over
twenty years later. Emotional ups and downs she must
have had. "Dorothy is at present suffering from the
most terrific depression I have ever witnessed," wrote
Pernel to Pippa in 1892. "She never speaks a word and
sits immersed in gloom all day long."

Duncan Grant says that the younger members of the
family were convinced that she had a love affair with
Sydney Foster, a married cousin. Possibly this was one
of the "intrigues of the most obvious and violent
nature" which were carried on under Lady Strachey's
nose, but evidence is lacking. The flirtations alluded to
in Dorothy's surviving letters are more commonplace.

At the time that she was being educated at Les
Ruches Dorothy had little or no contact with her next

sister Philippa; there is a great gulf fixed between ten and sixteen; but by the time Dorothy was twenty-six and Pippa twenty the gap had shrunk and almost vanished and they shared gossip, gaiety and beaux. They made their mother give evening at-homes at Lancaster Gate, they got up parties for subscription dances and they passed their young men from hand to hand. "Mama is in fits because Captain Nathan* is coming from Sept 8th to 10th," wrote Dorothy, "and I shan't be there and she is mortally afraid you won't be. But I hope you will and that you will be extremely fascinating and keep him in the family." Lady Strachey's alarm was all too well-founded.

"It is rather fearful being left alone with your young men!" she wrote to Pippa. "Mr Bond arrived on Wednesday . . . and Capt. Nathan is to be here on Saturday." Luckily Mr Bond was a croquet fan and the indefatigable Lady Strachey played matches with him until she "actually got a threatening of gout", fortunately staved off by the use of Blair's pills!

Dorothy seems to have had a large supply of young men, none of whom she took in the least seriously. There was one, who she alludes to as the "Unfortunate Evan", to whom she was always forgetting to write; there was Mr Crackanthorpe, "one of Cousin Minnie's crew of young men and exactly like all the others—youthful, weedy and with a squeaky voice"; there was "a youthful gunner by the name of Tomkins—not much older than Jimbeau. I told him that I could read people's characters from the shape of their heads and said that he was evidently the possessor of romantic

* Afterwards Sir Matthew Nathan, Governor of Queensland. He proposed to Dorothy.

and heroic virtues with a dash of equally heroic vices. He was highly delighted and asked for more!"

Dorothy's letters to Pippa, in short, display none of the charged emotional content of *Olivia* but are as high-spirited and girlish as those of any ordinary young woman. She was in some ways the most human of the Stracheys. "The blot on my existence is having to read to grandpapa," she wrote. "I simply loathe it and feel it is vile of me."

Among the younger members of the family Dorothy was closest to Lytton, in spite of the fourteen-year gap which divided them. He recorded that "Dorothy evening after evening in that room" (the Lancaster Gate drawing-room) "kissed me a hundred times, in a rapture of laughter and affection, counting her kisses, when I was six." When he was at school at Leamington and their parents were abroad she took it on herself to insist on his coming up to see a London dentist instead of having his teeth "removed by the dozen" by the local practitioner. Later on she shared his intellectual sympathies perhaps more than anyone else in the family. She wrote to him about Flaubert's letters, Greek verbs and Voltaire's tragedies. Finally, on February 8th, 1903, she wrote as follows:

"Dearest Lyt,

Please give me your fraternal blessing. I am going to marry Simon Bussy. Most people I am afraid will think it exceedingly wild, but in reality it is an action of the highest wisdom. (*vide* Maeterlinck.)

We shall only have 2d. a year but we shall be very gay and sensible—and live if possible in a minute house near Roquebrune."

Simon Bussy had originally entered the family as a friend of Pernel's, met while she was studying for her French Doctorate in Paris. She admired his pictures and Lady Strachey saw them on a visit to Paris and, as we have already seen, persuaded Sir Richard to buy one.* He seems then to have offered her a portrait of Pernel as a gift, and both pictures were highly appreciated. "Hurra! hurra! great joy and delight," Lady Strachey wrote. "Your Papa was just hurrying off to the City—late as usual—and could only stay to see your portrait uncovered; he was *very* much pleased, says it is a charming picture and exactly like you. Dorothy and I are delighted with it." This was in December 1899. A year later Dorothy wrote to Lytton, "Bussy the painter is staying in the house and I now talk French in my dreams. He is a charmer and amuses me intensely." She amplified the statement in a letter to Pippa. "The chief amusement at present is the visit of Bussy, who is established here with a room full of pictures. He is a sweet and charming person—though withal weird—and he amuses me intensely. We have long conversations on every mortal subject and I find the obscurity of a foreign language is a great help to freedom of intercourse. It is possible and even natural to say things in French that one would rather be dead than mention in English. He is very harrowing and piteous though poor little object and quite forlorn in London."

We do not know how long it took Dorothy to discover that Simon Bussy was what Plato describes as the "other half" for which she had been looking all her life. When she had convinced herself and him that this

* See page 25

was so there was a good deal of opposition to contend with from a family who certainly still looked on Bussy as "a poor little object". It is said that Lady Strachey was horrified to find him mopping up the gravy on his plate with bits of bread; nor could Mlle Souvestre, who was something of a snob, feel that the son of a cobbler was an eligible *parti*. Nevertheless Dorothy was thirty-seven and must be presumed to know her own mind. "You will doubtless be more astonished than pleased," Lady Strachey wrote to Lytton, "to hear that Dorothy is engaged to marry S. Bussy. She is very much bent on it, and of course must do as she chooses." She added a postscript "Oh la! la!" When the Strachey parents finally gave way, however, they did so not only with grace but with generosity. Sir Richard bought the Bussys a small villa called 'La Souco' at Roquebrune and Dorothy's assurance that they would be "very gay and sensible" on "2d. a year" was, in fact, fulfilled.

Once away from her family's immediate orbit she learned to cherish them dearly. Two years after her marriage she was writing to Lady Strachey: "It seems so dreadfully tantalising that you should be in Paris, darling Mama. How I should love to see you. To think that twelve hours in the train would bring you here. But I know you would come if you felt you could so I won't say any more except that I long with all my heart to see you." She signed herself: "Your loving and grateful child, Dorothy."

She was, however, amply compensated for the separation from her family and her country. "I am sometimes very homesick for all of you," she wrote, once again to Lady Strachey, "but my dear Simon is really very angelic and a great comfort. It makes all the difference in life to have a friend of one's very own."

If Dorothy sometimes felt herself isolated in the midst of her large family, Pippa, the next sister, was its fulcrum and central point. She was the sort of person to whom everyone turns in sickness and adversity. After Virginia Woolf's suicide her sister Vanessa Bell wrote to Philippa Strachey: "Don't give us up whatever happens. I think of you as someone I can come to—and *shall* come to one day—who will always understand and help." This sums up very well the general attitude towards Pippa. She *was* someone who would always understand and help. "Belovèd Pippa", as Dorothy used to call her, was the family prop and stay. She was Ralph's closest sister; Pernel's *alter ego*; she nursed Lytton through many of his complicated childhood and adolescent illnesses and was by his bedside when he died; Oliver wrote asking her to be Ruby's "shield and buckler" when the latter made her first intimidating introduction to the family; whenever there was illness or mourning she was summoned; "My dear angel and stand-by" was what Lady Strachey called her.

There was, however, nothing mawkish, nothing too good to be true, about Pippa Strachey. Leonard Woolf says that though he had never known anyone "more profoundly and universally a person of good will," yet, "she was entirely without the congenital vice of so many good-willers—sentimentality". He also states that "unlike her sisters, Dorothy, Pernel, and Marjorie, she was physically attractive and she faced life and human beings with a charming spontaneous warmth which was rare in the Strachey family".

Pippa was not at all pretty, as may be seen from her photographs and she had a peculiar (though very infectious) screeching laugh, but Leonard Woolf's assessment of her physical attractiveness is borne out by the number of people who fell in love with her. How far her own heart was ever touched it is difficult to say. Her deepest affections were probably given to Roger Fry. He was not eligible as he had a wife in an asylum and although he was very easily attracted by women he seems to have regarded Pippa more as a friend or a sister than as an *inamorata*. There is one rather ambiguous letter written in 1915 when she was over forty that suggests that their long friendship may have had a physical climax. "All that valley from the Williamsons to Menton seems to me to belong to you. I thought in my sleepy early morning fashion of how extraordinary you were. Yes, you have got rooted very deep somewhere which makes it so pleasant to lean against your trunk in the chequered shade my dear subsidiary olive tree. But I don't think you know quite how extravagant your generosity is, giving so much with the casual air of someone who gives one a light for one's cigarette. C'est pas banal tu sais. Anyhow I know that you gave me a kind of new belief in myself, in my power to create life around me, which I thought were gone altogether. I don't feel with you as though I was a useless encumbrance of the earth." One may make of this what one pleases; what is certain is that at the end of her life Philippa Strachey told a friend that she had never loved anyone very much (she referred obviously to being in love for no-one loved her friends and family more) but that she liked things "to be pleasant". Pleasantness, restraint, good manners—these were Strachey ideals.

Her friendship with Roger Fry came, of course, at a much later stage in her life and is really outside the family period covered by this study. When she was a young girl, living in Lancaster Gate, she seems to have been rather attracted by Arthur Melville, a painter of the Glasgow School, whose impressionistic colouring and technique she immensely admired. "My Melvillian picture has arrived," she wrote to Pernel in 1895. "It is the pride and delight of my heart and I cannot possibly attempt to describe how enraptured I am to have it; it consoles me for all the horrors of life and even growing old will not be torturesome in its society. The most awful thing my imagination can summon up is being so poor as to be obliged to pawn it. . . . It is just a bit of hillside with a beautiful skyline and a rosy cloud behind it; a little burn is brattling down the valley on the right and in the middle are two brilliant birch trees on a round tussock. The picture is very dark but it is so full of colour that when you look at it you feel as if something smooth and delicious were being poured all over you."

It was hanging opposite her bed when she died.

It was not only Melville's painting that Pippa found attractive. He sent her two tickets for his private view which she could not go to as she was abroad. "You can imagine my despair. . . . I gave up everything as lost when the very first Sunday I came back he appeared again!" She and Lady Strachey and Dorothy went to his studio and he walked home with them across the gardens and came to dinner and "evidently loved us". Hearing he had had influenza Lady Strachey with her usual good nature invited him to join the family at Westgate "and to our amazement he did it!!!!! . . . We all made bosom friends with him especially Jimbeau who spent the whole day in his company." Tactless little brother!

We do not know if Arthur Melville ever reciprocated the interest that Pippa took in him. The fact that he married one of her best friends, Ethel Croall, proves nothing, for nearly all Pippa's young men after proposing to her and being turned down, married someone else with remarkable celerity—very often a friend or relation. Ethel Croall does not seem a particularly happy choice since she was exceedingly neurotic and at one point declared that "as she could not penetrate the riddle of existence she did not care to live". She had a positive *schwärmerei* for Pippa and wrote her endless involved letters calling her "my princess". Her brother David was also deeply in love with Pippa though she never seems to have considered him very seriously. Nevertheless she liked the Croalls and spent a good deal of time with them. They perhaps provided a relief from the overriding intellectuality of the Stracheys. It is true that the latter, quite contrary to the Bloomsbury image, were keen on games. Lady Strachey was a first-class billiards player and all of them were devoted to croquet. "They play a mean and wildly exasperating game," wrote Rupert Brooke; and the lawns of the large country houses which Lady Strachey took every summer in the Home Counties were frequently enlivened by deafeningly shrill squabbles as the family disputed over rules and play.

Pippa, however, was fonder of sport than any of the others. It was surely she who was the moving spirit when she and Lytton took up skating and she started the family off on bicycling trips when this pastime became fashionable in the nineties. It must have been the bicycling that led her to order "a pair of black alpaca knickerbockers made with removable linings of nun's veiling!! Isn't it shocking?"

The Crolls provided, however, greater opportunities than the Stracheys could rise to. They took her sailing up the west coast of Scotland in small boats and they taught her to drive both tandem and four-in-hand. Her own relations were inclined to regard her engrossment with the Crolls with a slightly wry humour. "You really ought to have belonged to a hunting Squire family," wrote Lady Strachey apropos of the tandem driving; and her next letter starts: "May I humbly enquire when you propose to return home?" She adds teasingly: "There is some lovely news about your Papa [this was the bestowal of the gold medal from the Royal Society], but as you are not here and it is strictly confidential you will probably have to wait to see it in the papers." While Dorothy on another occasion wrote: "I was much relieved to get your letter as we had begun to think you had taken up your abode with the Cs for good. I was just going to write and sternly summon you to return as really it is too dull when you are not here and I am sure I am quite as likely to commit suicide as Ethel."

Although, as this letter shows, Dorothy and Pippa were close and congenial friends, Pippa's dearest sister was undoubtedly Pernel, only two years younger than herself. The long series of letters addressed "My darling Miss Joan," "Dearest Jye Pee", "My darling Penee", "My dearest Pen", stretch from the early nineties to Pernel's death in 1951. In contrast to the letters from Dorothy young men are hardly mentioned, though the

sisters seem to have taken a certain interest in clothes.
"Mrs Ercot," (presumably a dressmaker) wrote Pippa
to Pernel, "has done something *most* ingenious with the
spike in the bead collarette and also with great fussing
and excitement she . . . removed some little jet tails
from an ancient trimming of Mama's and sewed them
on to your evening body where you will see them in a
prominent position in front." They had to be careful
with their small allowances but one feels that the
Strachey sisters lacked dress sense.

One of the chief subjects of their correspondence was
music which was an overriding interest in both their
lives. They not only enjoyed and analysed an enormous
number of concerts but they both performed. Pernel
was a member of the Bach choir at Cambridge and
Pippa played first a recorder and then a contrabass
viol in the Dolmetsch ensemble. Her first fine enthusiasm for the latter, however, seems to have worn off.
"Pray don't speak to me of Dolmetsch," she wrote in
1896, "I have only practised once . . . and have
forgotten *everything*—even my notes—even my clef! One
of the strings is broken and I dare not write for a new
one for fear of reminding him of my existence as I know
I shall be nabbed the moment he hears from me! It is a
vicious circle. Shockingly vicious."

Pippa always had a slight sense of grievance that she
was the least well educated of the sisters and was left
to be the daughter at home. Her adolescence coincided
with an unfortunate moment in the Strachey finances.
Sir Richard had retired from the Indian Service when
it was still nominally the East Indian Company and it
was not till over twenty years later that the Government allowed him the full pension that would have

been his without question had he been in Government Service when he retired. Consequently her parents did not feel able to afford to send Pippa to Mlle Souvestre's, and owing to lack of proper coaching she failed for Cambridge. There is no denying that she was sad about this but she let no glimmer of her own disappointment cloud her letter to her younger sister when, after being coached by Dorothy for only eight weeks, Pernel passed her Little Go and entered Newnham. This provoked an explosion of family pride, Pippa reported. Sir Richard even broke out at the Meteorological Council and "lectured to the old boys upon your and Dorothy's prowess. They all listened aghast and George Darwin said: 'And this is the examination over which our young men are constantly plucked!' and Admiral Wharton said: 'Oh yes but everyone knows that Strachey's daughters—!!!' Clearly the person who gains most by your efforts is *me* who without doing a hand's turn or knowing Alpha from Omega am wafted aloft between you and Dorothy and perched on a pinacle [*sic*] where it only requires the exercise of a little adroitness to maintain myself. Ha! ha!!"

Obviously her family had some doubts about how Pernel would settle down in the then not very aristocratic atmosphere of Newnham. "Have you discovered any person you can talk to in a Christian manner?" asked Pippa. "Are most of them vulgaire and what do they think of *you*?" At the very beginning Pernel herself seems to have had her doubts. "In one minute and a half," she wrote to Pippa, "I have got to go to a hideous entertainment called a cocoa; you are given a spoonful of powdery cocoa and one spoonful of 'cow' that is to say condensed milk. These you mix together in a cup till they look like mud; boiling water is then poured on, the next process being to try and drink it. Weird cakes are also handed round. At ten o'clock at night this depresses me somewhat." But Cambridge was already beginning to weave its spell. "I am already attached to Cambridge," she wrote. "Until the wind carried off the leaves the Backs were a marvellous spectacle. The elms were all the same bright yellow and the ground was thickly covered with yellow leaves; there was a bright red beech in King's meadow which made you rejoice to see it. It is no good at all trying to describe it; you must come up here next October and see the sight."

In time she was to fit into Newnham, of which she became Principal in 1923, as a snail into its shell or as, in earlier days, a devout intelligent girl would have fitted into a nunnery. She was the most difficult of the Strachey sisters to get to know. In her early photographs her long narrow little face, with the inevitable spectacles, peers out between two thick bushes of hair, like some small woodland animal looking out of a thicket; in later prints she towers above her small sisters, her calm, sculptured eyelids giving her a resemblance to a Bellini Madonna. As far as we know her life was devoid of emotional complications. Like all the Stracheys she was devoted to her family; otherwise Cambridge, Women's Rights and music seem to have filled her life.

Marjorie, the youngest of the Strachey sisters, was very far from being a cloistered type like Pernel. She probably felt with Dorothy that the "sensual element was totally lacking from our upbringing". Certainly in 1913 when she was over thirty we read of her at one of the wilder Bloomsbury parties dancing "with nothing on but a miniature of the Prince Consort". As, unlike the rest of her thread-paper family, she was very large and fat, the spectacle cannot have been aesthetically pleasing. Another of her parlour tricks was to recite nursery rhymes without changing a word but in such a lecherous and suggestive fashion that her auditors either collapsed with laughter or were forced to leave the room in disgust.

But this was far in the future. In the Lancaster Gate days she was a schoolgirl with long hair flapping down her back, thumping out Gilbert and Sullivan on the piano, coming home from Allenswood with measles and making comic drawings of herself covered with spots, ragging with James in a way which caused Lady Strachey to make a dip in her even handwriting and to explain: "This is not locomotor-ataxy but the result of James and Marjorie struggling over my body."

Above all, her childhood and girlhood were absorbed by Lytton. He was only two years older than she was and in early days they were very close. In childhood they wrote to each other as husband and wife. From then on they were indefatigable in concocting plays, verses and poems. None of these are of great literary merit though *The Itchingham Letters* is plainly a foretaste of *Ermyntrude and Esmerelda*.

These effusions went on right up till 1901 when Lytton was twenty-one and Marjorie nineteen, but in time he naturally grew away from her emotionally, and outstripped her intellectually. In her biography of Chopin Marjorie lays great stress on the composer's relationship with his little sister. They acted plays and composed verses much as she and Lytton had done.

But Emilie died young and there was therefore no problem of a continuing relationship.

In some ways Marjorie was the odd man [or perhaps one should say the odd girl] out in the family. Lady Strachey with her overflowing bounty was devoted to all her children. Marjorie, possibly assailed by some momentary doubt, once said to her mother: "If you hadn't got ten children you would be quite rich." To which she replied: "And however rich I was I couldn't buy anything I liked better." It was an excellent answer and bears the stamp of truth, but there is no doubt that Marjorie held an unfortunate position in the family, between Lytton, Lady Strachey's most gifted and brilliant child, and James, the adored last-comer. It may be imagination but Lady Strachey's letters to Marjorie seem flatter and less interesting than those to her other children and Marjorie's replies are certainly shorter and duller than her sisters' letters.

She was much younger than the rest of her sisters and there is no doubt that they were closer to each other than they were to her. After she went down from Newnham Pernel taught for a while at Royal Holloway College near Egham, and there was a scare that she might have to take up residence there. "Isn't it terrible?" wrote Lady Strachey to Pippa. "Dorothy nearly cried at the suggestion and was not at all comforted when I suggested that Marjorie would be at home permanently."

Nor was Marjorie as intellectually distinguished as the rest of her family. Her novels are mediocre and though her romanticised women's magazine-like *Life of Chopin* was an American best-seller one cannot but think that the Stracheys must have read it with some distaste. Yet in some spheres she held her own. Although she did not get on particularly well with her mother she perhaps resembled Lady Strachey more closely than any of her other daughters, not only in her massive build but in her enthusiasm and geniality. Marjorie was malicious and had a sharp tongue but there were members of the closely knit Strachey circle who preferred her warmth and ardour to the rather aseptic benevolence of the rest of the family. She also had an undoubted gift for teaching which was surely inherited from Lady Strachey. It mattered little that she did not have the solid intellectual background of an expert and was at times only one lesson ahead of her pupils. Quentin Bell recalls her taking a course on the *Risorgimento*. "She came to each lesson bursting with newly acquired information, and the kind of information that you wouldn't find in most text books, a letter from Mrs Browning, a paragraph from *The Times*, a poem by Swinburne. Sometimes she was unable to keep this to herself.

"'My DEAR, do you *know* what that odious man Napoleon III said to Franz Josef at Villafranca?' (but one needs a special system of notation to record Strachey speech).

"No bloody nonsense about impartiality in Marjorie's teaching; she knew which side she was on and for her, the battle was still being fought while she talked about it."

With such stimulating gifts to offer her pupils, with the affection and concern which she felt for them (she seldom lost touch with them and followed up their future careers), with her great zest for life, it is perhaps unfair to describe Marjorie as frustrated, and in the purely sexual sense of the word this was certainly not so.* Yet although she always seemed to be having a good time and to be bubbling over with ideas and activities it is possible that very stridency showed that she wanted and needed something more. The impression remains that while Pippa and Pernel fitted perfectly into their roles of educated, independent, self-sufficient women, to whom an intellectual and civilised relationship with the rest of the world was all-important, there was something elemental about Marjorie which remained unsatisfied. She might have been happier had she, like her mother, married at eighteen and borne thirteen children.

* She is said to have had a passionate affair with Colonel 'Josh' Wedgwood, the well-known Liberal M.P. The story goes that before spending a week-end with him she felt impelled to confess or to boast to her mother. Lady Strachey strongly disapproved, whereupon Marjorie countered: "Well what about George Eliot?"

○ V ○

To most people the name Strachey connotes 'Bloomsbury' and the image called up would be the prim façades of Georgian London squares inhabited by rather freakish people with squeaky voices, who stood for pacifism, anti-Imperialism and culture. It cannot, however be sufficiently emphasised that, in fact, the Stracheys had their roots in Anglo-India and during the whole of the nineteenth century most members of the family lived and served there. It was only the younger Stracheys to whom India was no more than a background, something of which they must have been aware but had no impact on their daily lives. The last vital experience of it came in 1900 when Pippa, then aged twenty-eight, went out as a tourist to visit Ralph and to represent the family at Oliver's wedding to Ruby Mayer.

This was the turning point in Pippa's life. She left England an intelligent, affectionate, high-spirited girl, with a good deal to fill her life; music, relations, the neurotic and difficult Croalls, a host of small obligations; but also with a slight sense of unfulfilment. Compared with Dorothy and Pernel she was under-educated, she had no particular wish to get married, yet what else was there? She returned from India a woman knowing that she could cope and cope alone with the most difficult and trying situations, that she had great initiative, a talent for getting her own way and an almost unequalled power of persuasion. When she returned she was no longer to be just the daughter at home. She set about obtaining testimonials and became the Secretary of the Fawcett Society. In 1907 she organized the famous 'Mud March' in which women from all over England converged on Westminster demanding the Suffrage. In 1909, under a pseudonym, she wrote a one-act play in favour of Women's Rights which was produced at the Court Theatre in a double bill, the other author being Bernard Shaw.

She sailed, chaperoned by Uncle Trevor Grant, in the S.S. *Egypt* in October 1900. There were a great many of the Anglo-Indian Stracheys and Grants to keep her company. "We all send our love to you and Uncle Trevor," wrote her mother, "and the main body of the passengers on board, consisting I believe of our relatives." The most important of these were Sir Arthur Strachey and his wife Nellie. He was Pippa's first cousin although a good deal older than she was, and she soon became very fond of him. The other friend that she made on the voyage was an American girl, a Miss Hayes, with whom she shared her cabin. Pippa was a bit astonished to find that she was journeying to Baluchistan "to marry an unknown person she met years ago on a ship". However as, on further investigation, the fiancé (a soldier) was found to be a brother of William Archer (the translator of Ibsen) and exceedingly handsome, Pippa thought that Miss Hayes might be forgiven.

Once arrived in India Stracheys and Grants lay even more thickly upon the ground. Ralph was Chief Engineer at Lillaloah, a railway settlement just outside Calcutta, Oliver was in the Traffic Department at Dinapore near Allahabad, Dick was stationed in the hills at Rawalpindi. Pippa's first cousin, Arthur Strachey was Chief Justice of the North-Western Province, her cousin Jack was A.D.C. to the Lieu-tenant-Governor in Bengal, her uncle Charlie was at Simla, and so on and so on. Not only were the living members of the family in evidence; there were also the remains of past glories. The portrait of her grand-father, Sir John Peter Grant, stood on the stairs of Government House in Calcutta; the tablet put up by Lord Lytton to her uncle John Strachey confronted her among the marble and mosaics of the Fort at Agra; and when she visited a Moslem College at Aligarh in the North-West Province which John and Richard Strachey had administered for so long with so much success, she found that because of her name she was regarded with "awe and respect". The tra-dition, she wrote, was apparently extremely strong, "and even the little, tiny boys are imbued with it".

She began to be more and more conscious of her Anglo-Indian heritage. Like all children she must have heard a thousand stories of old times repeated again and again by her parents, but now all the faded glories, the long dead histories had come to life in her mind. "My dearest, darling Papa," she wrote, "your life will be made a burden to you with hundreds and thousands of questions on hundreds and thousands of topics so the best thing you can do is *at once* to begin a strong course of tonics to prepare you for the mo-ment of my appearance." She was the only one of the Strachey children who really loved India and if she had been a boy she might have been a notable ad-dition to the list of great Indian Civil Servants.

Pippa's Indian visit started with a catastrophe. She

fell ill with enteric fever. It was only a mild attack because T. H. Huxley had insisted she should be vaccinated but after that she succumbed to jaundice and, on top of all, she upset a boiling saucepan over herself. "We have been horror-struck to hear of your scalding accident," wrote Lady Strachey, "and feel like the Bennet's neighbours when Lydia eloped, that you are marked for misfortune."

Pippa recovered, however, in time to attend Oliver's wedding, and to convalesce by staying with Arthur and Nellie Strachey at Allahabad.

Arthur Strachey was an immensely clever, unconventional man, much loved by the Indians but regarded with some suspicion by his own compatriots. "What society in general thinks of him I can't imagine," wrote Pippa, "but my theory is that their whole energies are concentrated in the endeavour to reconcile his well-known 'cleverness' with his curiously freakish behaviour, which act being beyond their power they are reduced to bewilderment and gasping. I think they must consider him rather charming though, because he is so very good-natured."

Pippa had ample opportunity to perceive this last quality, because owing to the tiresome behaviour of her liver ("may its name be degraded") after jaundice, she was forced to stay on at Allahabad instead of returning to Ralph and the more unhealthy atmosphere of East Bengal.

It was during this visit that Queen Victoria died on January 1901. The emotional shock to India was not, of course, so great as it was to England, where everyone from top to bottom of the social scale felt as if they had lost not quite a mother but a presence, a protection, a bastion against Fate. "Nobody who has not seen it," wrote Lady Strachey, "can imagine what it is like to see every human woman in London in black." Nevertheless in India the death of the Queen-Empress was felt as a loss and not only by the British. "With one accord," wrote Pippa, "every single shop in the native town [of Allahabad] was shut up and in the evening all lights were extinguished and the streets perfectly deserted. All of this was quite spontaneous."

A minor but pressing problem was the question of mourning. "The wretched shops here hadn't *one* ready made black coat and skirt and 'durzies' (native tailors) are almost impossible to procure." Pippa had to content herself with a black riband round her hat, "a curious cape embroidered with wriggling patterns in horse hair", and an appeal for help to Dorothy and Lady Strachey. The two latter rose nobly to the occasion. Dorothy was particularly pleased with "a black chiffon hat with white rosettes to change . . . considering the enormous amount of work in it the price is moderate—35/-." It shows a commendable briskness on the part of all parties including the Indian mail, and also demonstrates the length of Victorian mourning, that the boxes arrived by March 27th and were in plenty of time for the remainder of Pippa's tour. The black clothes were only too appropriate for a different reason as yet unguessed at.

After a recuperative month with Arthur and Nellie Pippa was quite ready to start out on her travels.

On her arrival at Bombay she had been horrified to find that the East India Railway, of which her father was Chairman had made no arrangements to welcome her. Ralph, with the usual pusillanimity of the male, had declared it was quite out of the question to make any kind of fuss, but this was not good enough for Pippa. It was not long before she had annexed the Agent's own special coach, with a large salon enough to dance an eightsome reel and a large bath with a tub, which she proceeded to treat as her own property throughout the rest of her visit.

Her first visit was to Rawalpindi where she stayed with her brother Dick and his wife Grace; her second and far more exciting venture was Malakand to stay with her shipboard friend Miss Hayes, now Mrs Charles Archer. Malakand was one of the most inaccessible of the frontier posts and since the Afghan War of 1897 practically no women had been allowed in the fort where the whole garrison was perpetually on the *qui vive* for an Afghan attack.

Pippa spent a blissful week there in the midst of "a wild and confused mass of tents, packing cases, out-of-door fireplaces and ovens, heaps of firewood, mules, kerosene, oil tins, biscuit dittos, forage—every sort of object you can possibly imagine dumped down vaguely on the rocks and girded in with a stone wall and wire entanglement. From the Archer's [*sic*] house you look down on the whole of this extraordinary spectacle—the snowy peaks, the high hills, the valley, the Kopjes, the forts, the enclosure and you stand clinging to the verandah railing for fear of tumbling head over heels into the middle of it all."

From Malakand she travelled down to Simla to stay once more with Arthur and Nellie. When she got there, however, she found her cousin very ill with a blend of enteric and Malta fever, and she had been there less than a week when he died.

Everything now fell on Pippa. Nellie was in a state of shock, and Hugh Barnes, Arthur's brother-in-law,* who might have been expected to make all arrangements was at loggerheads with the doctor. Hugh was furious that he had not been told of Arthur's danger and the doctor "exhausted with fatigue & anxiety & general misery obviously considered this the last straw". Later Pippa managed to reconcile them in her very characteristic way. "When the hour of the funeral was fixed," she wrote, "I pretended to have too many things to do and pushing pens and paper in front of him innocently asked Hugh to send the note to the doctor for me. He did it with no remark and an expression of countenance which I was too much occupied to notice. I think it mollified the other creature and they get on perfectly now."

All had to be decided quickly for funerals in India cannot wait and there was one great difficulty. Arthur had left it in his will that he was to be cremated and Nellie, half-hysterical, was determined that his wishes should be carried out. This was beyond the comprehension of the British Raj at Simla. Cremation was a native custom, it was undignified, indecent and could not be allowed. Pippa was certainly not going to stand for this. She wasted no time in argument but went straight to the top, to the Viceroy himself, the formidable Lord Curzon, who, when the circumstances were explained to him, said: "If that was his wish, cremate him of course." The following evening the gun-carriage with the Union Jack on it wound its way to the Viceregal chapel. Nellie was too ill to come, and the little procession consisted of Pippa in her

* His first wife had been Arthur's sister.

rickshaw, the doctor and Hugh Barnes; not one member of the shocked society of Simla followed the coffin. However, as they passed Viceregal Lodge, the gates swung open and there stood Lord Curzon in black with a top hat followed by his military attaché. Pippa stopped the procession and motioned him to take the place of honour behind the coffin but he waved her on and joined in just behind the rickshaw.

In the chapel itself there was a sound of scuffling and Pippa turning round saw the verger refusing entry to Sir Arthur's devoted Indian bearer Tulsi. She stamped down the aisle and insisted on his admittance.

The coffin stayed in the chapel all night and next day came the question of the cremation. Pippa entrusted it to Tulsi, explaining to him that his master had paid India the greatest possible compliment in wishing to be cremated after the Indian manner and that he, Tulsi, must undertake it. The poor man seemed rather overwhelmed by the task but she insisted and sat down to wait for him in the church porch while the body was removed. After two and a half hours he returned, shrugged his shoulders and emitted the one word: "Can't." "Nonsense," said Pippa, "of course you can. You do this every day for your own countrymen."

He disappeared and there was another long pause. When he came again it was with a horror-struck face and carrying a long, untidy brown-paper parcel. Luckily the doctor had come to look for Pippa and appeared at this moment. He uttered an exclamation, turned her round so that she could see no more, walked her briskly to his house which was nearby, saying to his wife: "Give her some strong tea!" and vanished. The ashes later appeared, disposed of neatly in a casket.

Meanwhile Nellie had suffered a complete collapse and was only kept alive on champagne and morphia. After four days the doctor pronounced her out of danger but she still had to be nursed through a long and tedious nervous breakdown. The doctor insisted that she should leave Castle Grove with all its sad associations but houses were few and far between in the season at Simla and there had to be two moves, all the anxiety falling on Pippa. The second house they found had been let to the Maharajah of Jeypore and it took three days solid whitewashing, scrubbing and disinfecting by an army of about twenty servants led by Pippa before they could move in.

The next duty that Pippa had to undertake was to go down to Allahabad to clear out the house, pack up some of the furniture, sell the remainder, and collect Arthur's personal effects and papers. It was still the hot season but the new Chief Justice was due to come in and it was a task that could not be postponed. Hugh Barnes, reared in the tradition of the helpless memsahib, was horrified that she should go down alone with no better protection than Tulsi but she laughed at him.

It was not only a responsible but rather a heart-rending job. "The servants and people are all very sweet. They were discharged about 6 weeks ago but they all turn up in motley garments and perform any duties they consider suitable. . . . They really are touching and I am very sorry for them poor things. . . . Arthur's loss appears to be very much felt. Tulsi says that wherever he appears he is surrounded by people in mourning and I am told that even in the districts the natives knew his name and reputation and believed in the High Court because he was at its head. . . . When you know something about the composition of the High Court here you are able to perceive the tragedy for the country. It's to be hoped that Stanley will be a decent judge but he knows nothing whatever about natives and not one single word of Hindustani."

On the last day Pippa sent for all the servants and gave them parting presents from Nellie making a separate speech to each one, "translated by Tulsi into exquisite flowing periods". This was painful enough but the worst of all was at the moment of departure. "The platform was crowded with people pressing around the railway carriage and making speeches and sending messages to the Lady Sahib. There were some of the old servants who were really heart-broken. One poor old syce (groom), I believe the first man Arthur engaged in India, who had known the family always and who always called Arthur the 'butcha' (child), was perfectly desperate. . . . The whole scene at the railway station I shall never forget. It was a curious experience to have had to represent the family in this way."

When she returned to Simla Pippa found Nellie very much better but one more obstacle remained to be surmounted. Several of her letters to her mother during this period had been marked private but this one was headed:

PRIVATE & CONFIDENTIAL
Please burn with speed.   So DANGEROUS
that it might with advantage
be burnt before it is read.

The reason for all this to-do was a ridiculous argument that had sprung up about the disposal of Arthur's ashes. His widow was naturally anxious to take them to England and have them buried in the family plot at Chew Magna in Somerset. Arthur's parents,* however, who had never much approved of Nellie, were frantically and neurotically anxious that the ashes should be left in India. Pippa suspected that this was because they feared Nellie might come to Florence, where they lived, on her way home and bring the casket with her. Pippa, always administratively capable, arranged for a friend of the family going on leave to take delivery of the ashes and convey them straight to England—but the irritation and ill-feeling caused by the Stracheys' unkind letters, coupled with nervous fatigue, left her exhausted; and after Nellie's departure for Europe she managed to snatch a few precious days holiday all by herself.

This perhaps is the place to speak of her rickshaw and of Azerat Ram; both featured largely in her Indian travels. She had bought the rickshaw in Lillaloah and when she arrived in Simla she found to her great joy that Nellie had engaged for her "five (5) (most people have 4 and some degraded beings 3) delightful retainers exquisitely arranged in beautiful new serge suits and putties [sic], brown leather belts and white puggaries [sic] with scarlet painted tops and scarlet and gold bands across". The head man or 'mate', Azerat Ram, represented that he was a Brahmin of very high caste, a claim which Pippa took with a grain

* Sir John and Lady Strachey. Sir John was Sir Richard's younger brother and had been one of the best Governors of the Punjab.

of salt but which later turned out to be justified. He was of a very pugnacious temperament. On one occasion he had a row with a cabman and appeared, as Pippa put it, "in his true colours as a man of blood". She was forced to intervene and told him that "it was against the 'dastur' of Memsahibs to have these affairs carried on in their presence". He said that "he knew fighting was not pleasing to me but as for him it was the *one* pleasure of his life. He would fight every day and all day if he could have his desire. He was a Goorkha and better than 10 of the men of Hindustan. If ten men came he would be glad to kill them all— if 100 men came he would be glad and kill as many as he could and then die himself. He was thoroughly exalted and began to talk about his Kukri as if it had been Excalibur itself."

In spite of this little episode, Pippa was devoted to Azerat Ram and it was under his guidance that she set out in her rickshaw attended by her five *jampanis* for her trip among the hills. Hugh Barnes thought she was mad but the doctor quite approved. He must have realized that her mind and body both needed the solace of complete change of scene and of solitude. It worked perfectly. "Everything is delightful," she wrote, "no difficulties of any sort and complete peace and happiness in the sun with snowy hills to look at and fir trees to sniff." When she reached the first *dâk* bungalow, she was so tired she went straight to bed and slept for two and a half hours and woke just in time for a "slight stroll before darkness came on. It was so heavenly that I said to myself: 'No matter what may happen in the remainder of the tour—legs may be broken or any other fearful misfortune may occur and still I shall consider myself amply repaid by this one evening.' "

Pippa spent a week in the hills, camping and walking and riding in her rickshaw, carrying on long conversation with Azerat Ram in her elementary Hindustani. They discussed "high philosophical matters" she told her family and exchanged information about the supernatural. He told her about Hindu witches and *shaitans* (devils) and she retorted with the fairies who seemed to fill him with surprise and amusement. The expedition set her up both in body and spirit and it was a welcome break before she returned to Simla and from thence to Lillaloah.

During this time Ralph Strachey had become engaged to a girl he had long courted called Margaret Severs and Pippa was naturally to be a bridesmaid at the wedding. She had never met her future sister-in-law and when she did it does not seem to have been very felicitous. She obviously tried very hard to be just and kind but Ralph was her special brother and the words "not good enough for him" lurk between all the lines describing Margaret. The best that she can find to say is that she is "absolutely straightforward and thoroughly ladylike".

The wedding took place on October 29 and after the bride and groom had left there was a most uproarious party. "Nearly all the creatures were railway people and knew each other intimately so that they had no scruples about playing the fool . . . they all made speeches and proposed each other's healths in the most idiotic terms. They made a terrific shindy but were rather entertaining so I threw myself into the thick of the fray and drank my own health with much enthusiasm. The other females thought it too dangerous and remained seated in a group solemnly conversing." The party ended with a sing-song to "Oliver's accompaniment on the seat of a chair. . . . I must say that there's something rather pathetic about them. They are so strangely childlike and simple that you can't help liking them. This is what Willoughby (Huddlestone) calls a Wild Spree and will be spoken of for many years to come as one of the most delightful days of their lives."

After the wedding Pippa once more set off on her travels. She had hoped for Uncle Trevor as a companion but this did not work out and she therefore set forth accompanied only by Azaret Ram and enjoyed herself enormously. She did the usual tourist's round of Agra, Fatehpur Sikhri, Jeypore, Udaipur, Ajmer, Delhi, etc. All travel letters describing sight-seeing strongly resemble each other so that there is no need to transcribe Pippa's impressions though it throws an interesting light on the state of Anglo-Indian culture when she remarks: "The people of this country consider me *raving* to be amused by the sights but I simply love them."

She returned for a family Christmas and a round of Calcutta gaieties to Lillaloah and then paid a farewell visit to Oliver and Ruby at Dinapore. There is no doubt which sister-in-law she preferred. Margaret, she wrote, "looked very handsome at the Drawing-Room and made the most elegant curtseys. She has a beautiful figure and swept along in her train with immense grandeur." But her encomiums on Ruby are far warmer. "The more I see of Ruby the more fond I become of her. She is *very* pretty indeed and dresses charmingly and it is a sweet sight to see her with her babe.* I consider Oliver's situation thoroughly satisfactory. Both adore one another and both are charming creatures."

Pippa's thoughts were now turning towards home. She had been away for a year and three months. Nevertheless, she was loath to quit India. "I *believe*," she wrote, "that the shiny East has cast its glamour upon me for ever more . . . but in spite of all I cannot exist for many more days without seeing you all again. I am longing to embrace you every one and am already going mad with excitement at the thought."

The voyage home was made in a German ship which put in at Naples, since Pippa wanted to stop off at Florence for a day or two to see Uncle John and Aunt Kate and Nellie. Among the welcoming band was Willoughby Huddleston whom she had left at the 'Wild Spree' after Ralph's wedding. He had come by the quicker P. & O. and had lingered in Italy to meet her. He was very much in love with her and she was fond of him. Lady Strachey hoped for the match but Pippa refused him. Possibly she felt a future of small stations along the railway diversified by an occasional Wild Spree was not enough!

The Stracheys, including Nellie who was now quite robust, were overjoyed to see Pippa. "The crisis," she wrote (presumably the dispute over the ashes), "is now over—all parties have risen from their beds, but the strain is terrific. . . . The relief of having an outsider to make conversation is obvious." For the first two days she felt "like an middle-aged gentleman in a novel by Anthony Hope . . . life carried on in a

* Julia Frances Strachey had arrived.

succession of tête-à-têtes of vital importance and concerning affairs which to say the least of it are no business of mine".

Her arrival was, she felt, though it seems absurd to say so, a godsend, but she grudged every minute away from Lancaster Gate. At last, on Monday, March 24th she was able to write that she was leaving the next day and would arrive at Charing Cross on Thursday afternoon at 4.55 p.m. "I am wildly excited and counting the minutes but there still seem a good many of them—to be exact the number is 3052 without making any allowance for the lateness of the train!"

So Pippa came home to Lancaster Gate and, in the course of a few years, all her brothers followed her, They had never fitted so happily into India as their forbears; they were not quite of the same calibre and their work was less demanding, less responsible and less exacting. Nevertheless they both gave something to and gained something from their adopted country. The Strachey view of service in India (and this was not only true of the Stracheys but of the Lawrences, the Grants, the Plowdens, the Ritchies and hundreds of other Anglo-Indian families) may have been paternalistic, perhaps even a shade patronising (as was their attitude to most of the rest of the world) but it did have the redeeming grace that they loved the country and the people. One has only to contrast Pippa's great fondness for Azerat Ram, Arthur Strachey's desire to be cremated in accordance with the custom of the country, Ralph, competing with his bearer in a choice flow of vernacular epithets when they drove the pony cart through the crowded suburb of Howrah, with the attitude of their compatriots, the residents at Simla, who would not go to Arthur's funeral, who tried to turn away his bearer from the chapel door, who thought Pippa's desire to see the monuments of India "raving madness", to realise how much things were changing for the worse. It seems significant that the Chief Justice appointed to succeed Arthur Strachey knew "not one word of Hindustani". One can almost hear the the rustle of a page of history as it turns.

○ VI ○

The Stracheys had, of course, a large circle of distinguished friends; Joachim and Piatti among musicians, among literary figures, Browning, Tennyson, the Carlyles and George Eliot, and among scientists George Darwin, Tyndall, Lubbock, Galton and Huxley. The children were perhaps not greatly concerned in these relationships. They must, of course, have sat on the knees of a great many famous men. Pippa describes how, at the age of five or six, she was taken to the Athenæum by her father. He whisked her up a very long flight of stairs, past the porter who made faint gestures of dissent, and deposited her "in a small room with a big fire burning and beside it a gentleman sank down in a leather chair reading a book. 'Oh Huxley,' said my father with his head through the door, 'look after this child will you, for a few minutes. I want to go and speak to—' And he pushed me in and shut the door behind me—'How de do?' said the gentleman. 'How de do?' said I, walking up, and we shook hands. He had thick, dark hair partly grey with a great lock hanging over his forehead, and a very nice brown face with deep-set eyes and shaggy eyebrows like my father and many of his friends. So when he asked me to sit on his knee I accepted. 'Would you like me to be a cockatoo?' said he. 'Yes,' said I, and then he ran his fingers through his forelock and made it stand straight up in a tuft, and he put on a cockatoo's face and a cockatoo's voice in which the rest of the con-

95

versation was conducted . . . it was very enjoyable, and when my father came back I eagerly told him what was going on. Professor Huxley grinned and said he sometimes amused his own children in that way, and smoothed down his hair."

Such was Pippa's first meeting with the great Huxley and it was probably also the only time that any lady guest had penetrated the sanctum of the Athenæum.

But young people do not on the whole take great stock of their elders, however important. Dorothy wrote: "As for the people who came to the house, many of them were highly distinguished, we admired them without listening to them. Their world seemed hardly to impinge on ours."

There were, of course, plenty of their own contemporaries who were to become reasonably well known in their turn. The other boys had gone to India so early that the young men were mostly supplied by Lytton's and James's Cambridge friends, the Keynes brothers, Rupert Brooke, Saxon Sydney-Turner, Leonard Woolf and of course the Stephens.

The Stephens, who had many Anglo-Indian connections, must have long been acquaintances of the Stracheys but the friendship does not really seem to have ripened till Lytton was up at Cambridge with Thoby. The first mention that we find of them in Lady Strachey's correspondence is in 1901 when both families had taken houses in the New Forest for the summer. "Vanessa and Virginia drove over," she wrote, "and Mr Stephen and Thoby walked and were very late. The two girls looked very pretty and were rather shy I think; your Cousin Minnie found a great

deal of fault with them, merely I believe on the general
ground that the friends of the family ought to be
discouraged. Mr Stephen is very deaf and I had to
speak into his ear-trumpet, but he is so conversible
that there was no difficulty at all." This was the
occasion on which Lady Strachey was in high feather
having discovered among the books in their furnished
house a first edition of Ben Jonson. Virginia Woolf
remembered her thrusting it in front of Lesley Stephen
and pointing out the inscription: "*Ex dono auctoris*".
"My father looked and admired, but a little grimly
I thought and on the way home he said to me: 'I
didn't like to tell Lady Strachey, but the accent
should be on the second syllable of *auctoris*, not the
first!' " It seems rather a chilling reception to what
was, after all, a very considerable literary find, but
luckily Lady Strachey seems to have noticed nothing!

Cousin Minnie's* reaction to the Stephens visit was
a typically Strachey one. Lady Strachey herself with
her overflowing generosity and hospitality can certainly not be accused of a similar narrow-mindedness,
but with her, too, it was very much a case of 'family
first'. Her eldest daughter Elinor wrote of "her love,
her reverence one might almost call it, of the family
as an entity. It may have been partly owing to the
Scottish blood that ran in her veins, but her warm-
hearted interest extended from her own children and
their belongings to every member of the very large
circle of our connections on both father's and mother's
side, and she remained its centre until her death."
Lytton, too, wrote of the Sunday afternoon at-homes
at Lancaster Gate when "the drawing-room gradually

* She was Mrs Elton, a first cousin of Sir Richard's.

grew thick with aunts and uncles, cousins and connections, with Stracheys, Grants, Rendels, Plowdens,
Battens, Ridpaths, Rowes". If Lady Strachey had
ever aspired to be a successful *mondaine* hostess, and
there is no evidence that she ever did though she was
perfectly capable of being one, the aspiration would
have foundered on this family rock. For who could
have managed a successful salon where one was likely
to meet Aunt Henrietta Grant who had been dropped
on her head in childhood or Uncle William Strachey who
wore the same kind of suits, with innumerable buttons,
that he might have worn at Holland House in 1840?
Kindness of heart and social success do not, alas, mix.

The dearest of Lady Strachey's relations was, however, what was known in Victorian days as perfectly
'sortable'. This was her elder sister, Elinor, Lady
Colvile. Lady Colvile was far less intellectual and
intelligent than Lady Strachey. Dorothy remembered
"interminable and heated discussions, in which my
mother was invariably in the right and my aunt
beyond belief inconsequent and passionate". On the
other hand Aunt Lell, as the children called her, was,
according to Dorothy, "sensitive to art to the very
finger-tips of her beautiful hands, and created about
herself an atmosphere of '*ordre et beauté, luxe, calme et
volupté*' ". It was, of course, easier for her in that she
was a rich childless widow (she had had one son who
died young) with a house in Park Lane, another in
Gloucestershire and a villa in Mentone. In earlier
days she had sheltered the elder Strachey children while
their parents were still in India and her nephews and
nieces were very fond of her, amusing themselves by
imagining her in the most incongrous situations. Pippa

wrote from India that she had asked Ralph to guess who was coming out to stay at Lillaloah "to which he replied without a second's hesitation 'Aunt Lell!' It is a splendid idea and I have visions of her strolling in her Chinese garment among the trees and palm trees." And in Pernel's early days at Newnham Pippa inquired if the other students didn't find her guests "rather peculiar", adding, "Aunt Lell is clamouring to go and see you and she would be the finishing touch!"

Aunt Henrietta or Hennie was peculiar in a different way. While her mother, Lady Grant, was still alive Aunt Hennie shared the charming house on Chiswick Mall to which the former had retired. The old lady used to read the novels of Jane Austen aloud to her daughter one after another and then started to go through the canon afresh. This was Aunt Hennie's great delight and she would every now and then stop the reader to ask, for instance, why Emma said such and such a thing to Mr Churchill.

After Lady Grant's death Lady Strachey, on whom most of the practical work of the family devolved, had to find other accommodation for Aunt Hennie. She found her a home at Marlborough with some ladies who seemed "truly kind and most anxious to make her happy". But the parting was a sad one. "I must say my heart bled for the poor creature," Lady Strachey wrote. "She was very sad but tries hard to be brave. It was a pity the change could not have been made from Aunt Elinor's, as she enjoys herself so very much when she is with me. . . . I gave her an exquisite ruby and diamond brooch (originally worth 4/6 but sold off at 6d.) which went a little way towards consoling her."

Aunt Hennie was however in no sense 'put away' and used to come for long visits to both Lady Colvile and Lady Strachey. "Aunt Henrietta was suddenly seized with inspiration," wrote Lady Strachey in the course of one of these, "and spent the whole of yesterday writing with feverish speed; the result was two novels, a play and a poem. *We* have now to read them." Her nephews and nieces delighted in her comments. "She . . . remarked that it was very wicked to cut off dogs' and horses' tails," wrote Pernel to Pippa. " 'When an intelligent creature like God orders them to be there why should men cut them off?' " She also in the course of some remarks on the beauty of the Messiah said: "It was so delightful the way the chorus turned over the leaves of their music all together!" Although they laughed at her they did it gently and it was as much a pleasure to her as to them when they persuaded her that she was the Secretary of a very important Committee for the Protection of Fish.

The Stracheys were also well supplied with uncles, three on their father's side, two on their mother's. Of these the most eccentric was undoubtedly Uncle William Strachey, who, although his Indian career only lasted for five years, chose for the rest of his life to keep 'Calcutta time', rising in the late afternoon and going to bed with the sun. "Who should turn up this afternoon," wrote Dorothy from Syston Court, one of the Stracheys' rented summer houses, "but Uncle William! I was all alone and had to give him his breakfast (6.30 p.m.)." Once upon a time, in an effort to sustain a more normal time-table he had bought a mechanical bed at the Paris Exhibition which upset the occupant at any appointed hour of the morning. Using it for the first time he was thrown out into his bath, standing next the bed, and, in a rage, smashed the bed and the clock and resumed his old habits.

The most pervasive of the uncles was Uncle Trevor Grant. He was Lady Strachey's favourite brother and, since the days when she had been locked up in a small room with her uneaten tapioca pudding and he had climbed in through the window and chivalrously consumed it for her, they had been as she put it "the greatest chums". Uncle Trevor, who had once been in the Indian Civil Service, had married a Miss Clementina Gouldsbury who suffered from the drawback outlined by Kipling in *Plain Tales from the Hills*. "But—but—but— Well she was a *very* sweet girl and very pious, but for many reasons she was 'impossible'. Quite so. All good Mammas know what 'impossible' means. . . . The opal-tinted onyx at the base of her finger nails said this as plainly as print."

Aunt Clementina was dead by the time the Stracheys came to live in Lancaster Gate and the five sons of the marriage never seem to have been allowed to come home from India. One of them had disposed of himself by getting hugged to death by a bear; the others remained in India, probably having posts in the railway service. One of them once came to England for a short time, bringing a wife with him, and Duncan Grant remembers being sent to Victoria to see them off with a spare pound in his pocket but strict injunctions not to give it to them unless they were short of money for their ticket. "Apparently they just had enough," he wrote, "but I shall never forgive myself for not handing the pound over to them. I suppose it was fear of Uncle Trevor." It is significant that during her Indian trip, although she travelled out with Uncle Trevor, Pippa never seems to have laid eyes on any of her Grant cousins.

However badly he may have treated his own children he was more than devoted to his Strachey nephews and nieces. The former regarded him with rather modified enthusiasm. "He's rather trying in some ways," wrote Lytton. "He makes the most disgusting swilling and squelching noises when he's eating and I sometimes feel I shall shriek if it goes on a second longer. . . . The truth is that he is a vagabond, not an ordinary civilized human being accustomed to live in houses, behave at table and so on. He ignores all that, and floats dimly on in his self-centred way. Sometimes I see him at dusk prowling along the seashore in his long flapping overcoat—a mystic solitary figure. What can he be thinking of? His sons? His photography? Old Indian days? Clementina? Death? Nothing at all? . . ."

His nieces, however, were very fond of him and he was most generous to them—family letters record a violin for Marjorie, a "wee bookcase" for Pernel; Pippa, however, was his favourite "he was seldom without his arm round Pippa's waist when he visited Lancaster Gate". His great devotion was to Lady Strachey. He was taken very ill in Switzerland in 1907 and she went out to visit him. "This is glory! great glory!" he exclaimed, and again: "This is better than any dreams, far better." He was thought to be dying but he seems to have recovered and to have lived on to be well over eighty.

Uncles and aunts as the Stracheys knew them have

almost passed away. There is scarcely a child of the
present day who has experienced the presence of
those strange, individual, frightening, eccentric relations who used to prowl around the outskirts of
family life. Nowadays they would seem to us intolerable; in those days they were regarded as inevitable or even enjoyable. Lady Strachey, for instance, loved to claim cousinship with the most
distant branches of the family tree. "She made me
feel, even as a child," wrote Elinor Rendel, "that I
belonged to a little world of our own, that I was a
member of a community whose doings, both past
and present, were infinitely interesting."

The little world flourished most vigorously during
the twenty-odd years that the Stracheys lived in
Lancaster Gate. After Sir Richard died in 1908 and
the house was sold Lady Strachey moved her depleted
family, consisting of Pippa, Lytton and Marjorie,
with Pernel and James in the vacations, to Belsize Park
Gardens in Hampstead. One gets the impression that
this was never a very happy house—not only because
of the 1914-18 war but because of family strains and
stresses. Lady Strachey's continued habit of reading
jokes from *Tit-bits* and kindred publications aloud at
meal times irritated her children almost beyond
bearing. Marjorie had a loud raucous voice and
squabbled with her mother. "How unfortunate it is,"
Lytton wrote to James, "that the only woman who
behaves with decency and propriety in the house is
Pippa, and that she's never in it."

In 1921 the family moved once more, to 51 Gordon
Square and re-established itself with Lytton, who
now lived mostly in the country, in a self-contained

flat, and with the Bussys, who frequently came over from France, perching on the top floor. One of the most endearingly characteristic stories of Lady Strachey belongs to this period. A new young parlourmaid, perhaps overwhelmed by the flow of talk and argument proceeding at the Strachey dinner-table, stood in the hall for a few minutes to collect her bearings. The dining-room door opened and Lady Strachey appeared. In the semi-darkness she mistook the maid's white cap for the head of Venus di Milo which also glimmered dimly in the half-light, and leant her elbow upon it. The girl was too petrified to move and, after a few minutes of quiet reflection, Lady Strachey, sighing gently, adjusted her false teeth and returned to the company.

The younger generation were now moving into the centre of the stage. Lytton published *Eminent Victorians* in 1918, Pippa was organising the Fawcett Society, Pernel became Principal of Newnham, and James travelled to Vienna to study psychoanalysis, thus laying the foundation for his monumental work of translating and interpreting Freud. But Lady Strachey still lived on, almost blind now, but indomitably courageous. Virginia Woolf described the last time she saw her. It was a summer evening and as Virginia and Leonard strolled through Gordon Square they saw Lady Strachey at a window and waved up at her, she was too blind to see them but someone must have told her who they were because "she strode at once out on to the balcony, leant over and flung her arms open as if she were embracing us. It was extraordinarily moving—very dramatic and yet perfectly simple."

THE STRACHEYS

Lady Strachey died in her sleep on December 18th, 1928. The family still held together after she had gone, it was still a tribal and talkative society, but its ethos had changed. The old Anglo-Indian atmosphere which was an essential part of Lancaster Gate; the musical evenings; the hodge-podge of uncles, aunts and cousins, had vanished for ever. The new generation was perhaps equally eccentric but infinitely more self-conscious. Bayswater had given way to Bloomsbury.

THE BENSONS

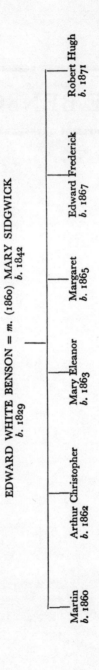

EDWARD WHITE BENSON = *m.* (1860) MARY SIDGWICK
b. 1829   *b.* 1842

Martin
b. 1860

Arthur Christopher
b. 1862

Mary Eleanor
b. 1863

Margaret
b. 1865

Edward Frederick
b. 1867

Robert Hugh
b. 1871

o 𝕀 o

Edward White Benson, Archbishop of Canterbury, might stand to us as the very archetype of a Victorian. The term is, of course, far too loosely used. Early Victorians differ from Mid-Victorians, and Mid-Victorians were quite unlike their sophisticated, questioning children of the late eighties and nineties; but when we speak of 'a Victorian' we tend to think of a Mid-Victorian and Benson, born in 1829, headmaster of Wellington in 1859, bishop of Truro in 1876 and Archbishop of Canterbury in 1883, fits exactly into that period. (The Queen herself, who was born nine years earlier than Benson, was also a typical Mid-Victorian.) The Archbishop had the Mid-Victorian virtues: intellectual and physical energy, devotion to duty, unswerving rectitude and sincere religious feeling. The qualities he lacked included imagination and the power of putting himself into another's place. He was unceasingly strenuous, vital, dogmatic and domineering and from early on he had armed himself with the triple authority of paterfamilias, schoolmaster and priest.

He had been left fatherless at the age of fourteen and from that moment considered himself the head of the family. His mother had wished to carry on her husband's business (he had been an inventor and had sunk all his small capital into a manufactory for white lead) but Edward refused to allow it. It would, he represented, ruin his sisters' prospects and gravely impair his own future in the Church. When his mother

died and it was found that her only means of sub-
sistence had been an annuity, uncles and cousins rallied
round to support the orphan children (there were six
of them), but even there Edward showed a remarkable
degree of intransigence. His mother's brother, a Mr
Baker, offered to adopt the youngest boy and make him
his heir. But Mr Baker was a Unitarian; it is true that
he conceded that the child should remain in the
Church of England, but the elder brother would have
none of it. It is characteristic that he seems hardly to
have considered the proposition from his brother's
point of view. His argument is far more concerned with
his own spiritual position. "I shall constantly hereafter
as a Priest of the English Church," he wrote in an
immensely long letter, ". . . proclaim 'Glory to the
Father and to the Son and to the Holy Ghost'. I shall
offer humble prayers to my Redeemer. . . . I shall
conclude every Service, every discourse, with ascrip-
tions of praise to Him with the Father and the Holy
Ghost." How could he do this with a clear conscience,
he asks, if "in one person's case, I had robbed the
Divine Persons of the worship and the praise that
should have proceeded from his heart, his mind, his
lips, his whole life"? The I's flash through the sentences
like telegraph poles.

Edward Benson's own future career was salvaged
from the family catastrophe in a curious way. He was,
at the time of his mother's death, at Trinity, Cambridge, where he had obtained a sub-sizarship. The
Bursar of Trinity, Mr Henry Martin, took a great
fancy to the ardent good-looking boy and offered to
pay all his fees and support him till he could earn his
own living. Martin furnished new rooms in college for

his protégé, took him on tours and reading parties, and even put by £500 for each of the sisters' dowries. In our time only one interpretation would be put on such generosity, and surely some lingering, adolescent, romantic love mingled in Mr Martin's heart with the desire for the son whom he had never had; yet in the mid-nineteenth century the friendship seems to have astonished no-one. It continued after Benson's marriage. Henry Martin was always a valued friend and honoured guest, the eldest child was named after him, but it seems that the younger man began to find the older one a little tiresome, a little over-affectionate. Mrs Benson, so much more sympathetic, so much quicker on the psychological draw, wrote in her diary for 1862 when all three were making a tour in Northern France: "Ed's feelings as to Mr M's demonstrations wrong, I thought and think quite wrong, but it was holiday weariness . . .—it past [sic]—did Mr M. ever know?"

This entry is very typical in that it shows Mrs Benson's intense awareness of other people's feelings and the Archbishop's complete ignorance of them. Although he himself was extraordinarily sensitive to the opinion of others, so that if he thought that affection or approbation was withheld from him he withdrew under a cloud of black depression, he seems never to have been aware of two-way traffic or to have grasped how blighting was his own disfavour. He knew that he had a violent temper and in his early days at Wellington as a young headmaster, only just thirty, dealing with a heterogeneous crowd of boys in a school devoid of tradition, he consciously traded on it. The accounts of his floggings, even taking into consideration that this was the heroic age of the cane and the birch, are horrific.

"He had a violent temper," wrote one of his pupils, "he would turn perfectly white sometimes when flogging a boy," and General Sir Ian Hamilton in his *Memoirs* recalled that for many weeks Dr Benson had flogged him every day (for being late in school): "When I went to the bathing lake and stripped I became the cynosure and stupor of the crowd. The blues of the previous week had changed to green and yellow, whilst along the ribs under my arm—where the point of the cane curled—the stripes were dark purple."

Benson repented of this in later life: "Without gentleness things may be done," he wrote in 1878, "but oh, at what needless cost of tears and of blood too," but he probably never realised how blighting an effect his displeasure, without any addition of physical violence, could produce. His children, on whom he never laid a finger, felt this strongly. "He was extremely sensitive," wrote Arthur Benson, "and . . . a careless word from one of us, some tiny instance of childish selfishness or lack of affection might distress him out of all proportion. He would brood over such things, make himself unhappy, and at the same time feel it was his duty to correct what he felt to be a dangerous tendency. . . . We feared his displeasure very much but we could never be sure what would provoke it. . . . I did not talk of the things that were in my own mind but of the things I thought would please him."

Fred Benson has the same story to tell. "He brought great and formidable guns to bear on small faults, which could just as efficiently have been visited with a light instead of a heavy hand. . . . And since the lives of small children, especially if they are vividly inclined, are a chessboard of small faults, this fear of the rebuke . . . became a constant anxiety to us, making us smooth-faced, blue-eyed dolls in his presence, with set fixed movements and expressions and when released from it, we scampered off as if from an examination under a magnifying glass."

Moreover, it was extremely difficult for the small, wriggling creatures under the glass to escape the all-seeing eye. It was omnipresent at school: "An open door, a crust on the gravel, a cap in the cloister, the transgressions of a dormitory man—he noted them all." It was omnipresent at home: "He had a very quick eye for the smallest things," wrote Arthur Benson, "and we never know if the private arrangements of one's plate would not catch his eye. If one ate untidily, or saved a particular bit for a *bonne bouche*, or made a little rampart of potato to dam up the gravy, he was sure to detect and remark on it."

His wrath was overwhelming. Fred, at his private school, organized a dormitory feast which was discovered owing to the sticky residue of Turkish delight upon the sheets. His headmaster said that he had been very naughty and hoped he wouldn't be naughty again but when his report reached his father it was a different story. "Had I committed the most heinous of moral crimes my father could not have made a blacker summing-up. He said that he would not see me among the rest of his children. I was to have my meals alone and disgraced upstairs, and to take no part in their games or their society." As this episode shows, Bishop Benson did not discriminate between mortal and venial sin. When Hugh Benson was accused of grave cruelty to another boy at Eton and nearly flogged for it* he was of course almost "paralyzed in mind" by his father's indignation yet he was, he says, "conscious of a faint relief in the knowledge that even if I were guilty . . . my father could not possibly be angrier with me than he had been, for instance, when I threw stones at the goldfish in the pond or played with my fingers during prayers".

This complete lack of proportion (Benson truly thought that a slovenly-rolled umbrella would lead to careless habits and on to moral heedlessness which would jeopardise both the owner's prospects in this life and his future salvation), made him unduly anxious over his children and obscured his very real love for them, causing it, as Hugh put it, "to be felt as heat rather than light". His great joy was in family life; he loved to have his children all around him at holiday time, working or reading while he worked on his *Life of Cyprian*. His family referred to these gatherings as "the Cotter's Saturday Night", and, as they were quick to realise, it was a game that must be played according to the leading player's rules. If he had finished his chapter or felt the need of a little relaxation they might talk, but he himself was on no account to be interrupted.

One of Edward Benson's most estranging qualities was the black despair that occasionally settled upon him. He was subject to intense neurasthenia and when he was in one of his melancholias it was impossible to please him. His wrath flared up on the slightest pretext and the dark tide of his depression communicated

* The matter was gone into and he was cleared.

itself to all his surroundings. All his children inherited this potent sense of misery, and perhaps it was not Benson's fault that the gloom he engendered had to be shared by all around him; nevertheless, it made living close to him a very uncomfortable business.

Another of his least lovable characteristics was the power he had of killing stone dead any pleasure of which he did not quite approve. Arthur Benson recounts two incidents of this sort. Once as a very small boy he was racing round the garden at Wellington, singing and blowing an imaginary trumpet. His father, who was writing in the summerhouse, called to him and said: "That is not quite the right way to behave on Sunday, is it, old boy?" The child's joy, of course, fell to the ground like a stone.

A little later Arthur, who was instinctively musical, got up very early and crept downstairs to try out some chords on the piano. His father, already up, appeared in the doorway. There was no reproach about disturbing the household. All he said was: "Hadn't you better read a useful book?" and all Arthur's incipient interest and joy in music fled for years. Besides recording this incident in his book of memoirs, *The Trefoil*, A. C. Benson introduces it into his first, partly autobiographical, novel, *Memoirs of Arthur Hamilton*. There he also tells another story. The little Arthur in the novel writes on a piece of paper, "I hate papa", and buries it in the garden. This does not find its way into the autobiography but it has the ring of truth.

There was another barrier of a seemingly more superficial kind, but which yet played a large part in dividing the Archbishop from his children, and that was the extreme delight that Benson took in forms of worship. Nothing perhaps has so much changed since the nineteenth century than the attitude towards the services of the Church. To Edward White Benson as to Charlotte Mary Yonge, long services in parish church or cathedral were an absolute refreshment and delight, at times almost a dangerous intoxication. The Archbishop had made himself a private oratory at the age of eleven and his schoolboy correspondence with his friends is full of descriptions of services, the keeping of Canonical Hours, etc. Even at the end of Victoria's reign this attitude was beginning to change. Fred Benson, describing Sundays at Addington, with their four services interspersed with readings from George Herbert and the *Pilgrim's Progress*, says that: "No shoal of relaxation emerged for a moment from the roaring devotional flood; if at meals the conversation became too secular it was brought back into appropriate channels; there was even a set of special graces before and after meals to be used on Sundays. . . . That day," Fred concludes, "for us was one of crushing boredom and unutterable fatigue."

The Archbishop's account of one of these Sunday afternoons shows how far he was from understanding his children's attitudes. "Maggie, Fred, Hugh and I," he wrote in his diary on August 10th, 1884, "went out in the shade." (There was an enormous cedar on the lawn at Addington beneath which these family gatherings took place.) "Hugh read the *Life of Paul the Hermit* aloud . . . and we concluded that it was *right* and necessary for the weal of Christianity, that such an awful enterprise as the desert life should be entered on in such an age of Sin and Delight as the Alexandrine life exhibited. . . . That being settled we discussed what was meant by 'getting one's own living' if one was rich in estates already, and concluded that ἀρχαιοπλουτεία (ancestral wealth) meant nothing but that God paid us our wages direct, and began by anticipation, so that our station and duty had to be much more rigorously consulted and lived up to than in any other case. We terrified ourselves by the memories of the Hermit Crab and the Sacculina, as exhibiting how frightfully we get punished, if we dare to live without working in body and spirit, and that Degeneracy is an almost intolerable vengeance on Degeneration. Then Fred read Stanley's account of Jerusalem as it was and is, but alas by this time I fell asleep under a tree and did not hear all."

Fred's account of a similar occasion when he was reading aloud from the *Lives of the Saints* makes an amusing pendant. Observing that not only the Archbishop but all his brothers and sisters had dozed off, he "read a few sentences of the page that had already been read . . . turned over 100 pages and droned a paragraph about a perfectly different saint . . . gave them a little more from the introduction, then in case anyone happened to be awake read the concluding sentences of the chapter about St Francis and stopped.

"The cessation of voice caused Nellie to awake and, with an astounding hypocrisy subsequently brought home to her, she exclaimed:

" 'Oh! how interesting.'

"Her voice aroused my father. There we all were sitting under the cedar reading about St Francis. Hugh had awoke, Maggie had awoke: it was a peaceful devotional Sunday afternoon.

" 'Wonderful!' he said. 'Is that the end, Fred?'

" 'Yes, that's all,' said Fred."

In many ways, of course, the children immensely admired their father. "We were proud of my father," wrote Arthur Benson, "proud of being his children, profoundly convinced that he could do everything better than anyone else." Nor were they indifferent to the worldly consequence his rapid advancement brought them. When the news of Truro filtered through to the schoolroom Maggie and Fred, then aged twelve and ten, skipped about muttering under their breath: "The Lord Bishop of Truro, the Lord Bishop of Truro." At Lambeth and Addington the perks were even greater. The two large houses, the stables full of riding horses, the policeman holding up the traffic when one rode with the Archbishop, the contacts with Royalty, all these were pleasurable. The Bensons, like nearly all Victorians, were snobs, and there is no doubt that they much enjoyed these things.

In later life, moreover, their relationship with their father improved. He became more mellow, they were more capable of standing on their own feet. But, with the possible exception of Martin, his eldest and favourite child, who died too young to leave memoirs, there is no doubt that he blighted their childhood. Yet the word is perhaps wrongly chosen. No-one who has not experienced some taste of Victorian family life (for it survived in places well into the twentieth century) can quite understand the extraordinary sense of living under the domination of one of those vital, strong-willed tyrants. If the tyranny be accompanied, as it frequently was, with vivid personality and wide ranging intellectual interests there was an excitement about it which is incommunicable. The best image might be that of a lowering evening sky occasionally showing rifts of pure gold made brighter by the encircling gloom. The immense and undying influence that Edward Benson had on his children is shown by the fact that he figured continually in the dreams of both Arthur and Hugh, as a dominating and vivid personality, twenty years after his death.

"We did not like Benson. Nobody did. . . . But everyone in the school loved Mrs Benson. She was very lovely* and young and made everyone feel happy."

Such were the recollections of a pupil at Wellington and the same story is borne out on all sides. Her children adored her, giving her that complete confidence that they denied to their father; her female friends were devoted to her; as the years passed by her husband grew to lean more and more upon her. "Her life was bound up with his in a way which is seldom possible to a wife," wrote Arthur Benson in his life of his father. "There was not a single thought or plan or feeling that he did not share with her: and from first to last her whole life and energies were devoted to him. For many years she was his sole secretary. He consulted her about everything, depended on her judgment in a most unusual way, and wrote little for public utterance that he did not submit to her criticism." On the surface it appears to be one of those perfect Victorian marriages, the life-long felicity of which is often envied by the present generation. The real story is far more unusual and more interesting.

Many Victorians had the idea of 'educating' young

* This must be an exaggeration. She was a fat, square little thing, but she undoubtedly had charm. Young she certainly was; when she was first married she was younger than the eldest boys at Wellington.

girls to adorn the blessed position of their future wives.*
In artistic circles the chosen young woman was often of
a lower social class, a model or even a prostitute. This
would obviously not appeal to Edward Benson, a
clergyman and a schoolmaster; he selected for his
experiment his second cousin, Minnie Sidgwick, then a
child of eleven.

Her father, a clergyman, had died young, leaving a
family of five children, of which the most remarkable
was Henry Sidgwick, who founded the Society for
Psychical Research† and married Arthur Balfour's
sister Nora. Minnie was the youngest child and was
described somewhat disapprovingly by her mother as
"more volatile than the other children".

Mrs Sidgwick settled in Rugby in order to be near
her boys. After the break-up of the Benson orphan
household she had taken Ada Benson, the youngest
girl, to live with her and in 1852 Edward Benson,
having accepted the post of a classical master at Rugby
also came to form part of the household. He was then
an extraordinarily good-looking young man with long
fair hair, a very well-shaped, slightly curving nose and

---

* This, of course, was not a wholly Victorian concept. One
of the most notable exponents of the theory was Thomas Day,
the author of Sandford and Merton, who in the eighteenth
century brought up two orphans in the hope that one of them
would qualify. In spite of his rigorous training (he dropped hot
sealing wax on their bare arms to inculcate fortitude) neither did.

† This Society arose from a 'Ghost Society' founded by
Benson when he was at Cambridge. In later years, however, he
became disapproving about psychical phenomena. Nevertheless,
he and all his family had pronounced psychical tendencies. They
were great 'dreamers of dreams' and frequently saw apparitions.
Chesterton once said that Mrs Benson not only seemed to know
everyone who had ever seen a ghost, but every ghost as well.

large light blue eyes. Ian Hamilton rather unkindly adds that he had a very long back line and short legs like a dachshund; he usually preferred in consequence to be photographed sitting down and in all his later portraits he wears a long priestly robe. In 1852, however, before he was ordained, he used to attend Rugby Chapel in light pearl-grey trousers, a blue frock-coat, an expensive silk tie and a pair of lilac gloves. This splendidly dressed, beautiful, vital young man must have seemed immensely impressive to the small girl of eleven; and when he extorted her mother's permission (one gets the impression that Mrs Sidgwick was rather bulldozed into giving it) to speak to Minnie, now aged twelve, on The Subject, she was overwhelmed. The Archbishop's diary records the scene: "Let me try to recall each circumstance: the arm-chair in which I sat, how she sat as usual on my knee, a little fair girl of twelve with her earnest look and how I said that I wanted to speak to her of something serious, and then got quietly to the thing, and asked her if she thought it would ever come to pass that we should be married. Instantly, without a word, a rush of tears fell down her cheeks, and I really for the moment was afraid. I told her that it was often in my thoughts, and that I believed that I should never love anyone so much as I should love her if she grew up as it seemed likely. But that I thought her too young to make any promise, only I wished to say so much to her, and if she felt the same, she might promise years hence, but not now. She made no attempt to promise, and said nothing silly or childish, but affected me very much by quietly laying the ends of my handkerchief together and tying them in a knot, and quietly putting them into my hand. I asked her whether the thought had never struck her when she read 'The Princess' to me so constantly. 'Never,' she said. She would then turn the pages backward and forward and say again she wondered she had never thought of it, and again she would exclaim she never understood this passage and that till today. She could say it almost by heart: she repeated the words 'Love, children, happiness.' 'Two of these are mine now,' she said."

E. F. Benson, after quoting the above passage, refers to "this little authentic Victorian love story, so precise and fabulous with its readings out of Tennyson's 'Princess' and its adorable heroine of twelve years old", but to a modern reader it seems almost intolerable, with its heavy burden bound upon a child, and so the child herself felt it to be. Twenty years afterwards Minnie Benson underwent a sort of religious conversion and as a spiritual exercise she set down a backward view of her life in which the main events were mingled with prayers and ejaculatory invocations to God. The first entry is: "Mother rather feared than loved," and this short sentence sums up the worst of the situation. Could the child only have confided completely in her mother the strain would have been much less; as it was, the masterful lover and the mother to whom she felt she owed her duty struggled for predominance and tore the poor little girl apart. The extract continues:

Ed. coming fear of him—love? always a strain—never the love which casteth out fear.

.   .   .   .

Desire of pleasing E. because of fear of vexing him—and having pleased him being happy in other things than him.

.   .   .   .

E.'s disclosure—tears and emotion—why? no real thought abt. it after. *Really* I think it made me younger. I wouldn't allow any responsibility—here fatal want of confidence in my mother.

.   .   .   .

Through all this early period to trace this *shallow heart*—easily moved, easily grieved, bright and sunny if all went well. Self indulgent—fond of pleasing others.

.   .   .   .

A terrible time. Dreary, helpless—from the first the most fatal thing was the strain on my conscience and the position towards Edward and Mama. He had been allowed to tell me but was not allowed to speak but he *did*—and more hand-embrace—etc. all weights on my conscience—and which did I love best? it was not love that was growing for him.

Oh the 1000 difficulties and complications! I lacked courage to bear his dark looks—gloom—but I see now I *did not* love him.

.   .   .   .

Mama and Ed. both wanting my love—neither at all satisfied—utter misery.

.   .   .   .

Lessons with Ed.—so dreaded—architecture and physical geography.

.   .   .   .

I had to strain the truth to satisfy Ed. by expressions of love and often was not true to Mama—as to speaking—I was influenced too strongly by her, without really loving.

.   .   .   .

At last the great complication. Mama wanted me to tell her all that he said, without his knowing of my promise— I made a stand, and, I think, rightly. The 2 walks with Ed. to Tree."

[One of Edward's letters refers to himself as the "Sir Cradocke whom you 'kissed *once*' (x by 1,000,000,000,000,000) under the greenwood tree." The allusion is to 'The Boy and the Mantle' a ballad in Percy's *Reliques* which he had presumably read with Minnie.]

.   .   .   .

Settling about engagement and marriage. Still no *real* love, but influence. I knew not God and his influence was the strongest I knew.

.   .   .   .

Then towards March came engagement known—elation —sense of being interesting—daily letters, but alas! no *real* what I know now to be love. . . . Oh how unfit for marriage! I liked the sense of making him happy. . . . I was happiest when I knew E. happy and yet wasn't with him . . . like a child I read novels, and eat oranges in the face of mighty mysteries . . . no confidence with Mother —till last morning = night, so childishly, confidently, without stay or guide, though trusting in God . . . *only childish in understanding*, I married that June morning.

Those who blame the sexual freedom of the present day might perhaps spare a thought for those poor little Victorian brides, corralled like calves into a pen, quite unaware of what they had to face, quite incapable of enjoying it. It is hard not to blame Edward Benson but apart from the odious selfishness and lack of imagination shown by his spoiling of Minnie's childhood and adolescence he was perhaps also a victim of his time.

Before the engagement was formalised the constant letters they exchanged had been very dull and correct, schoolmasterish on his part, docile on hers. Here are two typical specimens. Edward to Minnie: "By the way you must remember that *so* with an adverb is properly used with *that* following it—and *not* independently as if it were synonymous with 'very'. For instance we ought not to say in *writing* at any rate, and even in speaking it is rather vulgar to say, 'The character of Scipio Africanus is *so* beautifully described by Dr Arnold.' Remember this; you have used it 5 times in your letter which otherwise is a very nice one." Minnie to Edward: "My dear Edward, Thank you very much for your nice interesting letter which, I assure you, it was a great pleasure to me to receive, especially as I had been hoping for it for some time."

Once the engagement, however, was formally announced Edward's tone changes completely. According to his diary, Benson had first decided to marry Minnie on her eleventh birthday. He was struck by her fondness for poetry, her affection for himself and her diligence "in reading books that I have mentioned to her, and in learning pieces of poetry which I have admired". "It is not strange," he concludes at the end of a very long and involved sentence in which he explains that he will not be able to marry for many years, that he is "fond (if not too fond) of little endearments", that he has a weakness for falling suddenly in love and has already gone too far more than once and might therefore "on some sudden occasion be led . . ." [here the diary breaks into cipher] "that I should have thought first of the possibility that some day dear little Minnie might become my wife."

The thought of Minnie then, had been "a remedy against sin" for seven years, and when the offer of the headmastership of Wellington made marriage possible and the end was in sight his letters begin to reflect his passionate feelings. "I love so dearly everything that comes from you that I can scarcely bear to put the old envelopes in the waste-paper basket. There's sentiment for you." He sets up her photograph against "a certain pillow that *now* swells up quite plump and innocent close by mine but won't do so long". He kisses her future pillow every night and he values himself the more "for that a pure, sweet English girl loves me so passionately".

His error was perhaps natural for Minnie, carried away by the desire to please him (for as she said she was happiest when she knew he was happy and yet wasn't with him), was also writing very loving letters. "My own darling love, My desire to see you is so great that I scarcely know what to do, I press my ring and that makes me better. I have kissed it too until I am almost astonished that the stones are not worn out."

"By this day week," Edward finally wrote, "we shall sleep in Paris, married life with its untried bliss will be a reality."

Reality came all too painfully to them both. We resume Minnie Benson's retrospective account of her early married life.

Wedding night—Folkstone [*sic*]—crossing—Oh how my heart sank—I daren't let it—no wonder—an utter child, with *no* stay on God. No real reference to Him in all my actions=danced and sang into matrimony, with a loving but exacting, a believing and therefore expecting spirit. 12 years older, much stronger, much more passionate!

and whom I didn't really love—I wonder I didn't go more wrong. . . .

Paris—the first hard word—abt. the washing—But let me try and think how hard it was for Ed.

He restrained his passionate nature for 7 years and then got *me*! this unloving, childish, weak unstable child! Ah God, pity him! misery—knowing that I felt nothing of what I knew people ought to feel.—Knowing how disappointing this must be to Ed., how evidently disappointed he was—trying to be rapturous—not succeeding —feeling so inexpressibly lonely and young, but *how* hard for him! full of all religious and emotional thoughts and yearnings—they had never woke in me. I have learnt about love through friendship. How I cried at Paris! poor lonely child, having lived in the present only, living in the present still. The nights! I can't think how I lived."

○ III ○

Even the most disastrous of honeymoons must end
some time and in July the young couple returned to
England. They went first to Mrs Sidgwick's house at
Rugby and Minnie records: "I would have died rather
than that anyone shd. have thought for a moment I
wasn't happy." They then proceeded to Wellington,
to the Master's Lodge which was at that time in the
North front of the College to the left of the great gate.
(The new Master's Lodge with its pitch-pine panelling
and pale lilac walls, remembered by all the children,
was not built till 1865.)

This must have been a very trying time for Edward
White Benson. It was the make or break moment of his
career. He was almost solely responsible for the welfare
of this new foundation, whose scholars were, many of
them, difficult and backward boys. He had trouble
with the catering (a painful incident is recorded when
one of the governors had lunch with the boys and
could not eat the beefsteak pie as it was so stringy!) and
he was often at loggerheads with his governing body on
more fundamental questions. In one of his black moods
he confided to an assistant master that he felt utterly
baffled. "His work here did not prosper. The Governors
as a body hostile and on the look-out for the first sign
of failure in his administration. Worse than all, the boys
he had to teach were so heavy and unintellectual, he
found the Sixth a dead weight which it was impossible
to bear up against. And here he burst into tears."

In his family life he was aware that he had no private means, that he was a husband and the father of a rapidly growing family, and that he was partly responsible for his younger brothers and sisters. He was also aware that he was married to a very young girl who had not much money sense. He was obviously afraid of her becoming something like the Child Wife of David Copperfield, but he was far from displaying the patience and kindness that David exercised towards silly little Dora.

"I was very bad about bills," Minnie confessed. "I *knew* it was the one thing he dreaded and disliked— but I disliked the doing of them, and dreaded the gloom they always brought and so, cowardly and improvident, I put them off and lived in the present." After the birth of her second son in 1862 she found she was £40 in debt. "E. couldn't forgive as thou forgivest," she wrote, "couldn't trust though he tried. I remember how hopeless I felt it." These extracts come from her retrospective diary in which she later wrote: "I thank thee Lord for blotting out the distinct memory of many painful walks and talks and so many new beginnings and so many painful resolutions." There still exists, however, a contemporary diary for 1862-63 which records some of these painful incidents and would often be funny if it were not so pitiful. For instance, in January 1862 there was an occasion on which a dress-maker had sent an unwanted 'body' which cost £5 more than the stipulated estimate. Edward reproached Minnie saying "that it was a duty to notice things of that kind even though they gave one trouble". He added the peculiarly annoying sentence that: "Some people shrank from things of an unpleasant nature especially if they had fat chins." "This," Minnie continued, "rather riled me," (and no wonder!) "and I got up quickly and said pettishly, I am afraid, 'I knew you would say something of that kind—I won't stay!' Ed. said in *perfect good temper* 'If you do, you won't see me again today.' "

The quarrel concluded with Edward reading the unfortunate girl a tremendous lecture about the duty of ordering a household. It was, he said, "a law of God that cleanliness and order should lead to godliness". He ended: "And now, Minnie, I think you need not be pettish with me." She took it like a perfect Victorian wife: "Indeed I ought not—he is kinder and kinder, and I always feel even when he speaks severely that he really does it *for my sake*."

She could still, however, be hurt and annoyed by him. A year later he made "some *very strong* remarks" about the antimacassars which, she admitted, certainly did need changing. "It destroys one's whole peace of mind to be spoken to in that way, if one thinks about it, and if one doesn't I suppose it does one no good. Ada was in the room too. I don't think he knows what effect his words produce."

As the above entry shows, the situation was not helped by the prolonged visits made by the Head-master's youngest sister Ada, who was not a harmonious element, having herself a good deal of the domineering Benson character. Nor were the visits from in-laws more successful than such occasions usually are. The first time that Mrs Sidgwick came to her daughter's new home was described by Minnie as "a very unhappy visit". At Christmas, 1861, she had to put up with "our difficult party and E.'s neuralgia". She "was glad when it ended".

In January 1862 her brothers Henry and Arthur came to stay. Edward was away and they indulged in a seance and table-turning—but alas, the next day Edward came back and was "very vexed and spoke very strongly". "I can't feel that it is so wrong when undertaken in a reverent spirit, anyhow I suppose it is over for me now and I *must* be content. . . . I laid awake a long time thinking about it, for Ed. seemed to me to speak harshly, and to expect a great deal of me."

And then there were the babies who arrived with relentless regularity. Martin in 1860, Arthur in 1862, Nellie in 1863, Maggie in 1865, Fred in 1867 and, after a gap of four years, Hugh in 1871. The Bensons seem to have been strangely undecided about their children's names. Margaret was a compromise between Bridget, her father's choice, and Agatha, her mother's. Hugh was at first known as Robin and perhaps the change was made after the move to Lincoln and its connexion with "little St Hugh", while Arthur Christopher was almost christened Joseph Thomas; no wonder that he felt that such a designation would have been "a grievous injury to my self-esteem".

In very early days the children regarded their father as a god-like creature who swept in and out of their lives "something shining and swift; an external object whirling along on an orbit as inconjecturable as those of the stars, and wholly uninteresting". He would sometimes do delightful and fascinating things like papering the nursery at Wellington with pictures from old illustrated papers, or drawing detailed sketches of Gothic castles and knights and towns. Once Fred was given a cup of milk to drink by his father and adjured to drink it slowly. He did so, heard a chink and found a shilling. But as they grew older fear, as we have seen, entered into the relationship; "he brought too heavy guns to bear on positions so lightly fortified as children's hearts". They could never be open with him or at ease and, though of course they did not realise it, their mother was precisely in the same position. With her from the beginning they enjoyed complete trust and confidence. Martin was to his mother "more like a devoted brother" than a son. Arthur wrote that "it was my mother who opened, one by one, the doors of life to me. I suppose she was really so near her own happy childhood that she knew by instinct what we were thinking and caring about." Maggie in her childish troubles used to go and lay her head on her mother's shoulder "not to confide so much as to get strength from loving contact and say, 'Oh, mamma!' to which the expected reply was 'Oh, Maggie!' and that was enough."

Yet however close and fundamental the love of a mother for her children may be it is not enough to fill a young, ardently seeking heart. Minnie Benson felt this herself. "Youth and general bonhomie made me good to the children," she wrote—"but no guiding principle."

The centre of her emotional life remained unfulfilled. There is only one instance of a possible heart flutter as regards the opposite sex. In July 1862 Charles Ridding, afterwards her eldest son's headmaster, came down to examine at Wellington. "*How* I liked him," Minnie wrote, "was even too excited—head easily upset— Strange to remember the feelings he inspired."

It was only a passing glimmer for there is no doubt

that her true emotional life lay with other women. Whether this was the result of the failure of the physical side of her marriage it is impossible to say. It is true that what she calls her "first friendship" occurred in 1857, two years before her marriage. "I fell in love with her," she writes in the retrospective diary, "and spent a great deal of time with her—and loved her über alle Massen" [above all measure]—but this may have been only the normal girlish *schwärmerei* of a sixteen-year-old. After marriage, however, the diary begins to be studded with female names. "Annie—she loved me—I led her into some beauty some truth—but what might I have done?" "Katie Meyer came in here—not as loving me much—but Phillie was with her, and did—Oh Lord thou has given me in some measure the gift of love." "Hastings—Oh that sweet time with Emily! how we drew together! Lord it was Thou teaching me how to love—'friend of my married life'—how I loved her! and so it came to an end, and we went home and my husband took me on his knee, and blessed God and prayed and I remember my heart sank within me and became as a stone—for duties stared me in the face."

It is not likely that Mrs Benson ever had physical relations with any of these beloveds. She probably did not even know that such a thing was possible, but it is quite certain that all her deep emotional contacts were with women. "I came to love through friendship," she once wrote and that is undoubtedly the truth. All through her life, till she reached her final emotional fulfilment with Lucy Tait, she was inspired and moved only by women.

Her first serious *affaire de cœur* took place in 1872,

when she was abroad in Germany. The previous years must have been very unhappy ones. She was extremely ill after the birth of Edward Frederick, her fifth child (five children in seven years and she was still only twenty-six). Then came a respite of four years, but Robert Hugh was born on November 8th, 1871, and his mother suffered what was obviously a severe nervous breakdown. She was unable to sleep, lost her sense of balance and at times her memory. She went to Scotland to try to recover and then on to the Wordsworths at Lincoln.

The Wordsworths were now close family friends of the Bensons. They had been staying at Wellington when Christopher Wordsworth (a nephew of the poet) received the offer of the Bishopric of Lincoln. He wrote to refuse it but Dr Benson, masterful as always, altered his mind for him and retrieved the letter from the outgoing post.

The Bishop of Lincoln was a scholarly, very High Church ecclesiastic, more at home in the third century than in his own times. Although Benson was very much more broad-minded, his interest in ecclesiastical minutiae, in ritual, in the Church fathers, endeared him to the older man who looked on him as a sort of supplementary son. Mrs Wordsworth and the daughters also became close friends. Minnie Benson wrote that she had been much attracted by Elizabeth Wordsworth and had thought that her feeling was returned but: "Oh my vanity! . . . I thought she was thinking of and looking at me when far other and nobler things occupied her." Whether these things were God or Edward Benson is not specified but it is certain that Miss Wordsworth (who later became Principal of Lady

Margaret Hall) did have a very great admiration for the Archbishop. One feels that had Minnie died at this point, Edward Benson would probably have married one of the Miss Wordsworths.

The friendship was greatly cemented by a long-remembered and congenial holiday at Whitby in 1869. "How we walked and talked," Minnie wrote recalling this holiday. "E. was so happy at the love poured out on him by them all—revelled in it—I was so glad." Even the children participated. After they returned to Wellington from Whitby his mother was going over with Martin the various causes for which they had to be thankful to God. "Yes," Martin replied gravely, "it has done me good to see the Bishop." From this time on the young married couple and their children were almost adopted by the Wordsworth family and the Miss Wordsworths wrote to Edward and Minnie as brother and sister.

It was therefore extremely natural that Minnie should go to Riseholme, the Bishop's Palace at Lincoln, to try to recuperate. She might have gained more advantage from it had she been allowed to stay longer —but Edward wanted her home for Speech Day. Both Mrs Wordsworth and the doctor thought she was far too weak to travel and she herself wrote that though she was getting on she could not sleep properly as yet. Nevertheless, the dominating Edward had his way and she travelled straight through to Wellington without even breaking the journey in London as had at one time been proposed. She wrote the Wordsworths a comical account of the journey entitled 'Adventures of A Timid Gentlewoman'. It was expressed in mock heroics peppered with down-to-earth comments from an unsympathetic husband.* As for example: "She is Alone!! yes Alone! and the train rattled and roared and ran. [So unusual for trains, Ed.]" She arrived at Wellington, according to this account, at eleven o'clock at night and was carried fainting over the threshold by 'the Buttons'.

She was in time for Speech Day but it is scarcely any wonder that she became even more seriously ill. This time it was Arthur Sidgwick who intervened. He was Minnie's favourite brother (she once borrowed £40 from him without telling Edward) and he seems to have been seriously alarmed by his sister's condition. So much so that he positively snatched her up and deposited her with her brother-in-law, Christopher Benson, who lived in Wiesbaden.

Christopher had been a cripple from his earliest years but had lately married Agnes Walker, the daughter of an Oxford professor. For some reason this had displeased his brother and there had been a family coolness, but now the Benson household in the quiet little German town seemed a suitable and respectable refuge, though Minnie was extremely anxious that things should be arranged on an adequate financial footing.

At first the change and relief seemed to do nothing but good. Minnie was for a time tormented by the idea that she might once more be pregnant "ought one to pray that it may not be so?", but by October this apprehension had passed away. She seems to have got on reasonably well with Chris and Agnes: the latter she felt might be an example to her. "She had forgotten

* That is to say, the interpolations are not really written by Edward but are Minnie's idea of what he might have written.

something the other day and the way she behaved when he reminded her of it somewhat sharply, gave me a twinge I can tell you." She thought over "the past very often though no longer despairingly", and when her husband wrote to tell her that Bishop Wordsworth had offered him the Chancellorship of the Diocese of Lincoln, and that there was a possibility of their all leaving Wellington, she replied with a letter which must have touched him. "Our first home—where we first *really* knew each other and where our love, deep enough always, has grown and deepened and strengthened year by year, though each year it seems impossible to love you more. . . . Dearest I was such a child when you married me that I fear, am afraid you must have had many sad moments."

But this is not the whole story. Among the amenities mentioned in the earlier letters are the delightful walks and expeditions in the forests around Wiesbaden and the presence of "Miss Hall, the lady boarder [who] is a *very* pleasant person—clever and bright and merry".

Minnie fell in love with Miss Hall. There is no other way to put it. Here is the extract from the retrospective diary. "Then I began to love Miss Hall—no wrong surely there—it was a complete fascination—partly my physical state—partly the continuous seeing of her— our exquisite walks. If I had loved God then *would it* have been so—could it be so now? I trust in God, NOT—Yet not one whit the less sweet need it be—I have learnt the consecration of friendship—gradually the bonds drew round—fascination possessed me then the other fault. Thou knowest I will not even write it— but, O God, forgive—*how* near we were to that."

Then came the question of whether she should

return home for Christmas. Her letters to her husband
dwell on her longing to see them all again and to be
reunited with her children, but she got her sister-in-law
to write, and was rather ashamed of having done so as
she Agnes disapproved. However Agnes did write as
follows: "It is far better that the matter should be
settled for uncertainty is so trying. Your recent letters
—the result I imagine of her having given too good an
account of herself—coupled with her own longings
have made her restless and restlessness of course retards
her progress."

Matters were not helped by what seems to have been
a sharp letter from Doctor Benson on the eternal
subject of money. "I am very much distressed," Minnie
wrote, "that you think I have been extravagant and I
am afraid the children's presents will have furthered
the idea—but let me explain—Those things I sent
Nelly and them are ridiculously cheap 2/- or 3/- in
all."

Naturally the uncertainty and the emotion made
her really ill once more and Miss Hall nursed her
through a recurrence of all the old symptoms. Her
divided heart caused her much misery. "I do try not to
be more unhappy than I can help," she wrote to her
husband in January 1873, "but my Dearest, I am
giving you so much pain and worry! and those dear
boys!"

Finally she had to return, not much better physically
than when she set out, and mentally even more unhappy and confused. There is one final entry in the
retrospective diary about Wiesbaden to which there is
no clue except what can be gathered from its own
contents.

I haven't gone and I can't fully into the way I wronged my dear ones here—I lost my head—and, blessed be Thy name O Lord, I came to grief. The letter—ah! my husband's pain—what he bore, how lovingly, how quietly —our *talk* my wilful misery—my letter to her. Ah Lord, how blind thou allowedest me to get.

Doctor Benson must also have been undergoing much mental misery. The move to Lincoln had taken place in his wife's absence and the family was now installed in the Chancery, a remarkable mediaeval house on the eastern side of the Close. After several days of picture hanging and furniture moving, Benson took the elder children on a long walk where they experienced a curious optical illusion. The revolving white sails of a windmill appeared above the crest of a hill and looking as if a great fountain were playing and and sending up successive jets. "But," wrote Arthur Benson, "there was something wrong about the walk. My father talked eagerly and continuously; yet when we came back, we all agreed there was something serious the matter. It was not till many years later that my father, talking to me about mental depression, said that the most acute and intolerable attack he had ever had was on a certain day just after we had arrived at Lincoln. He added, 'Perhaps you will remember that we saw a windmill, and thought it was a fountain?' I did indeed!"

The beginning of their life at Lincoln was not a happy time for the Bensons. Dr Benson, so long an unquestioned autocrat, now felt the thrall of coming under direct ecclesiastical authority. With Bishop Wordsworth he was altogether in harmony but he was not entirely at ease with the Dean, J. W. Blakesley. "I regarded him with awe," wrote Arthur Benson, "because I realised that my father, who seemed to us to possess a natural and unquestioned authority and dominion over all visible persons and institutions, actually regarded the Dean with deference and even involuntary submissiveness." Blakesley had a dry, keen, incisive mind* and was very critical of any new proposal or enthusiasm. Benson, returning home after a Chapter Meeting, described how adroitly and effectively the Dean had blocked all his proposals. "He contrived to make me appear both unpractical and sentimental." When Dean Blakesley died Benson, then Archbishop of Canterbury, wrote: "He did me much good, because I always determined to obey him in all Cathedral matters, however little I liked doing so."

It may be salutary to learn to obey but it is not always pleasant and Benson probably chafed a little. Nor was Mrs Benson's return an unmitigated success. She found Lincoln dull, her new acquaintances dreary and was even, she wrote, unsympathetic to the boys. "How they felt it!" "Then," she wrote—we are still quoting the retrospective diary—"came stirrings of the old love—Alice Swan—the old ungoverned desire—*how* I pleaded—and duly in the midst came Thy messenger, O Lord of Hosts, my beloved Tau—and I did

* He also had a sense of humour. On one occasion Benson borrowed a book, the eighth of twelve volumes. The Dean offered to send it down and in a short space the Deanery gardener arrived, bearing not one but twelve volumes wrapped in brown paper on a wheelbarrow. Benson apologised for the trouble he had given, he had only wanted one book. "Oh, I always do that, I don't like gaps in my sets. People sometimes forget to return a single volume—I don't say that you would—but they don't forget to return twelve."

not know her at first—played even with my human
love for her and hers for me—felt it coming—felt how
different places were when she was there—but played,
played and all the while Thou hadst sent her, and she
has led me to Thee."

Tau was a Mrs Mylne. Mr Mylne was a middle-aged
man who had taken orders late in life and had come as
a married student to the Theological College at
Lincoln. (Later he became Vicar of Addington.) His
wife was deeply religious on evangelical lines and it
was through her that Mrs Benson experienced what
can only be described as 'a conversion'. She had
apparently for some time felt the faith in which she had
been brought up, the solid road of churchmanship
which so satisfied her husband, to be insufficient. She
needed a more human, a more emotional approach to
God. "Thou of thine abundant, rich goodness gavest
me hours with my darling Tau—hours in the fulness of
the beauties of Thy creation—and as she spoke of the
love of Thee—I know it filled her heart to the brim
—and its peace was shed on me."

This peace was never to fail her for the rest of her
life but it did not immediately work miracles. She had
hoped, she wrote, that "when I became a Christian, he
[her husband] and I would be more in union. I didn't
do it *for* this God knows—but I did think this wd.
come with it—and finding it didn't I rebelled." "What
am I to do?" she asked herself. "*First* He thinks more
of little remarks, is more sensitive, more easily hurt
than I am. Therefore I must not think of *being at my
ease* but of suiting my ways of saying things to his
feelings—and this without a shadow of thinking my
ways better than his—*I* like them better—but then I

am sadly apt in my turn to despise people whose form of wit I think poor—and it is much the same."

"Let me think," she goes on, on a later page. "Economy, punctuality, tidiness—these I owe to him —and these I will steadily cultivate—I ought to try to *please* him more, and please God I will. I think I have got into the habit of merely grumbling, especially after a visit from any of my brothers, that his ways and thoughts and feelings weren't exactly suitable to me. I have expected that Xtianity would do away with necessity of *accommodating* myself to him."

There is something sad and chilling about such a conclusion yet from this time there is no doubt that the marriage (though it never became one of 'true minds') did improve. Edward Benson also played his part. In February, 1876, he organised a General Mission which excited great enthusiasm and seems to have touched the springs of his own religious being; and in March he wrote his wife an immensely long letter, it must have been well over eight pages, from which the following are extracts:

"I shall indeed as earnestly as I can pray for what you bid me pray for. But you know what self-condemnation I feel on the subject. While I have really and warmly believed, and thoroughly realised . . . the truths of the unseen and the persons of that world, as actually taking part in this, still (I know not yet fully *why*) the facts which gave me such happiness and strength in other ways have not till lately, if even now, reacted with proper force, on my temper, my pride, my resentment, my self government, or my opinion of myself. I have prayed for humility and sweetness always, yet I have not had before me the right ideal of character. . . . The lost ground I have to make up is aweful. It is therefore I who want your prayers, more than you mine." He goes on to a long exordium about the necessity of loving God through Christ. His viewpoint differed from Minnie's in this, that while she approached God through the love of human beings, he felt that "when the true love of God in Christ is actually at work there is not the least fear of our forgetting to love everyone in their proper place, only one must, I am certain, *begin* by loving *Him* above all persons and things." He concludes rather movingly: "Ah! I labour in wretched words—too dry for you to read—but true if only I could beat my music out. We must utterly try to give our children some idea of the *Love* of God, while they get on so well in the knowledge of God's ways— the two must go on together.

"I am afraid this is all very awkward—but it is a true endeavour to express how earnestly I will carry out your wishes. And *you* for me? The Persons of God— the Father—the Son—the Holy Ghost—the aweful Trinity in Unity—This is what we must both know and love—Then we have hope for ever.

With all love and prayer,

Your most affectionate husband,
E.W.B.

I send you my letter such as it is. It does not half express my meaning or my love, but I can't do better."

So these two deeply religious persons approaching God from different aspects drew together and made a conspicuous success of the next twenty years of their married life. Yet it was not perfection. Three years after the Archbishop's death Mrs Benson records that she told their daughter that she had always longed, all her life, "for *harmonious* life and all those years it had not been. . . . Her father felt it was a poor conception of mine—that it was a kind of longing for *comfortableness* and not specially worthy."

In spite of domestic difficulties and the unsympathetic Dean, Doctor Benson was an outstanding success at Lincoln. He not only revivified the Cathedral worship and services and opened a Theological College but he started night schools in the city for men and boys, which enjoyed a great success. Curiously enough he got on very well with the working class. He was often impatient and dogmatic with the educated, "but," writes Arthur Benson, "to the lengthy explanations of mechanics or labouring men he used to extend a patience which we as children often remarked upon; 'I like to hear him explain it in his own way,' he used to say."

When, therefore, the new see of Truro was detached from the diocese of Exeter Lord Beaconsfield, also doubtless bearing in mind that Benson was a man of sound Tory principles, had no hesitation in asking him to become the first bishop. There were a few of those ritual hesitations and askings for guidance common to all Victorian bishops, concluding as they nearly always did in acceptance of promotion, and in the summer of 1877 the whole family transferred from Lincoln to Cornwall.

There was of course no palace at Truro so the Benson family took over the Vicarage at Kenwyn, a mile outside the town, which was renamed Lis Escop (Bishop's Court) by its new tenant. It was a charming Queen Anne house looking down on the town, the

estuary and the distant hills towards Falmouth. The
children were enchanted with the change and all that
summer they roamed around the fields and woods,
collected birds' eggs and denizens for their aquarium,
going out in the summer nights to take wasps' nests
and to 'tree-sugar' for moths. They had all the pets
they could wish for; a collie, Watch, to whom they all,
including the Bishop, were devoted; guinea-pigs who
were christened by Maggie with exotic Mexican
names like Atahualpa and Ixtilxockitl, canaries, and
a tame goat who used to go for walks with the family.
Mrs Benson, at the beginning of her widowhood,
went to a retreat in Cornwall and wrote: "I went for
a lonely walk in the lovely sunlight, up the Idless
Valley, looking towards Kenwyn—such broken frag-
ments of radiant memories came all about—till I
could almost have expected, and *did* ask for Edward
and Martin and Nellie with Watch and the Kid to
come round the corner—O God! if they had."

At first the Bensons were not altogether happy with
the change. The climate of Truro with its humid
steamy languor did not agree with its new bishop.
His books grew mildewed and his engravings foxed and
at times he suffered from his characteristic black depressions. On one occasion when walking with Arthur
Benson he broke a long silence by remarking "with dark
gravity that the behaviour of one of his clergy was
killing him, that he would have to leave Cornwall".

Mrs Benson for her part regretted the friends she
had left behind at Lincoln, her beloved Tau and the
Wordsworth sisters and the ecstatic religious atmosphere of what Elizabeth Wordsworth called the "little
spiritual hothouse in Minster Yard".

"I have been so very wretched and so very rebellious," Minnie Benson wrote to Susan Wordsworth soon after her arrival at Truro. "Oh I know how dreadful it is! I had thought I was never going to be rebellious again. I wonder if *you* know, to whom I don't think Nature has given a rebellious heart what an awful inheritance it is—and so when a lovely life alters & one comes right away, down here where nothing is helpful and all is strange, and one's heart so sore—there comes wilfulness and one doesn't struggle and it lays hold." In time, however, they adjusted themselves.

For the Bishop, Truro was a challenge and his vital strenuous nature rose to meet it. It had been a sadly neglected part of the diocese of Exeter, full of dissent abounding in pathetic, lonely, elderly clergymen with no congregations and so ill-paid that they could scarcely support life. One of them confessed that he had rented a pew at the Wesleyan chapel and used to go there on Sunday evenings just to get a little warmth and company. Another had turned the Second Book of Chronicles into rhymed verse, paid for the printing and not sold a single copy. His study was full of the unbound sheets. The Bishop went the rounds of all of these and as one of them said: "Ah if I had had someone like your Lordship to give me a hand and a word of encouragement, and perhaps to speak to my people, it would have been different!"

The Bishop's great activity was, of course, the founding of Truro Cathedral. He threw all his energy, his taste for building, his love of ritual into this and in an amazingly short time the foundation stone was laid by the Prince of Wales and the following Sunday (May 23rd, 1880) the Bishop preached in the yet unfinished nave. "His face [was] pale with emotion," wrote one spectator, "and yet irradiated with the tenderest smile of hopefulness; he seemed like a man who had won a victory by prayer." It was well that he should have had this occupation and this triumph for two years earlier he had undergone the bitterest sorrow of his life.

The Bensons' eldest son—christened Martin after his father's old benefactor—had turned out an unusually gifted boy. A most moving and delightful picture of him is given in David Newsome's book *Godliness and Good Learning*, and he was certainly the most remarkable child of a remarkable family. He passed head of the list into College at Winchester in 1874, he won the Duncan history prize, the Sixth Book Essay prize with an essay on Mohammedanism, and in 1877 at seventeen only just failed to secure the Goddard Scholarship, the highest classical honour of the school. His parents adored him, especially his father. He was far less afraid of the Bishop than any of his other children and the letters they exchanged in the last eighteen months form almost a correspondence between equals. Their tastes were similar, they both loved poetry and architecture and tradition. Nor was Martin a prig. It is quite a relief to hear of his muttering to Arthur when they returned to their private school: "Twelve more weeks of this beastly place," and he once went into his classroom at Winchester with four little Japanese dolls attached to the strings of his shoelaces and proceeded gravely with his construing.

Curiously enough his relations with Arthur, his next brother only a year and a half younger, never seem to have been very close, although they shared a sitting-room and did most things together. Arthur wrote that Martin's intellectual attainments were above his head and that he, himself, was "fond of solitary pursuits". Both Martin's sisters however adored him, particularly the elder one Nellie. Her letters to him are charming. There is one in dog-Latin: "*Darlingus superbus. Tua cara sistera and pussera greta suas carus frater*". There are serious ones: "Martin, I am such a horrid girl, so cross and lazy, and you are *so* good. Was it very hard to you to try to get good for it is to me? You are so much nicer than you used to be. Was it your confirmation communion that did it? I wish you would tell me." There are also nonsense letters, one of which is unconsciously pathetic. "My own," Nellie wrote on October 25th, 1887, "the reason I put the year is that in the depth of your affectionate nature you may be induced to keep this letter till its pages become yellow with age, so that when you look back on it when you are a man you will feel the remembrance of childish days when we were all young and silly may bedew your noble cheek with tears."

To the little boys in the nursery he was, of course, nothing but a hazy, glamorous figure. Fred was penetrated by a sense of his courage and condescension when he offered to stay behind in a dark wood to search for a toy the child had dropped, and Hugh's letter to Arthur on the occasion of Martin's death is a perfect example of the well-tutored Victorian child who has not an idea what he is writing about. "My dear Arthur, Martin is dead," he wrote. "Martain [*sic*] is gone to hefen. . . . I am so happy that Martin is gone to Jesus Christ. I hope we shall all go to HIM very soon. He is Saint Martin now."

Martin White Benson died on February 13th, 1878.* He had been stricken down with aphasia and a partial paralysis while taking tea at a master's home on February 2nd. His father was sent for but he seemed to recover very quickly and the doctor was reassuring. Then came a relapse, his mother was telegraphed for, and both parents were by his bedside when he died. He could not speak but he was quite conscious and the Bishop gave him Holy Communion. "A few minutes before ten," the Bishop wrote in his long and moving account of Martin's death, "the heavy breathing passed away. It became quite soft. His lips gathered themselves nearly together, and it looked like a baby's mouth—so soft and sweet and small. . . . He breathed in soft little gentle sobs—and these ceased to come—and our Martin was gone to God."

The Bishop was shattered. Both his elder sons were struck by their first glimpse of him after the tragedy. "The sight of my father's pale and agonised face on the platform there [Winchester], under the flaring gas jets, first experience of the tragedies of life," wrote Arthur, and Fred, who was only ten, remembered fifty years later the sight of that face as Edward Benson stepped from the carriage into the lamplight on his return home to Truro.

* The cause of Martin's illness remains something of a mystery. An abscess, with or without meningitis, encephalitis (virus) or cerebral embolism are all possibilities but all these would be accompanied by severe headache, a symptom which is never mentioned. A subarachnoid haemorrhage (probably from congenital aneurism or a blood-vessel abnormality) is perhaps the most likely possibility.

For the first time one begins to feel completely in sympathy with Benson. The man who in 1857 had written to a friend who had lost both his parents: "I really feel little regret for lost friends," since "prayer for them is such an inestimable blessing and the thought of them, and belief that they have passed through such experiences . . . is so great a thought", now really began to sound the depths of human anguish. Mrs Benson, with her comparatively recent religious conversion and the serenity with which it sustained her, was able to take the blow in what was felt to be a more Christian fashion. "Be comforted for Martin," she wrote to the old family nurse, "He is in perfect peace, in wonderful joy, far happier than we could ever have made him. And what did we desire in our hearts but to make him happy? And now he will help us out of his perfect happiness. He died without a struggle—his pure and gentle spirit passed straight to God the Father, and now he is ours and with us more than ever. Ours now, in a way that nothing can take away."

"I am learning from my wife," the Bishop wrote, "to subdue the ever rising longing for his sweetness back again." "My dear wife is the mothers' example," he wrote in another letter, but he could not quite subdue his own rebellious heart, "As yet," he wrote, "though I feel the help of his present relation to me, yet I am distinctly conscious that the help of his life near us, his thoughts and his sweet and perfect example, were . . . a more living and stronger help to me than now. I hope that I shall be able to win more faith. But it takes *all* my confidence in his present to prevent me from murmuring."

THE BENSONS

He did his best to overcome his natural grief, his "blind love", as he called it in the beautiful epitaph which he wrote for Martin and caused to be placed in the cloisters of Winchester.

O Amor, O Pastor, qui quem Tibi legeris Agnum
Vitali tinguis Morte, sinuque foves,
Nos, qui tam dulces per Te reminiscimur annos,
*Duc, ubi non caeco detur Amore frui.**

He drew closer to Arthur, now his eldest son, taking him on expeditions to see cathedrals and talking to him far more freely of what was in his mind. (These expeditions were marred for Arthur by the fact that his father would always say Compline in their private sitting-room and the seventeen-year-old schoolboy was "in constant terror that the waiter would come in and find us on our knees".) He also tried to find in Hugh, his Benjamin, a substitute for his lost hopes, striking the inadequate child with dismay. (He felt he wrote later, "like a small china mug being filled out of a waterfall".)

Yet in spite of his satisfaction in his other children, in spite of the increasing happiness of his marriage and the glory of his Archbishopric, Benson never got over his eldest son's death.

On his sixtieth birthday he confided to his diary that: "Martin's death remains an inexplicable grief—every day—to see into that will be worth doing," and

* O Love, O Shepherd, who touchest with living death and doth cherish in Thy bosom the lamb that Thou hast chosen for thine own; lead us, who through Thee remember such happy years, to where we may enjoy love that is not blind.

a few days later he wrote a poem which he showed to
no-one. The first verse goes:

> *The Martins are back to cornice and eaves,*
> *Fresh from the glassy sea;*
> *The Martin of Martins my soul bereaves*
> *Flying no more to me.*

and the last two run:—

> *. . . when he went home*
> *He carried my heart from me.*
> *Half I remain. Ere Martinmas come*
> *Go with this message from me.*
>
> *Say, "thou Prince, he is wholly Thine!*
> *Sent once on a message to me;*
> *Yet suffer me soon, at morning shine,*
> *To see him on Thy roof-tree!"*

∘ V ∘

Had Martin lived what would have become of him? One must remember that he was only half a Benson. One part of him was Sidgwick (he was said to be very like his Uncle Henry) and he had something of their probing, questioning minds. His religious faith was unusually strong, but then religious faith is often at its zenith in the mid-teens. Had he gone on to Cambridge, had he come under the influence of such a man as Leslie Stephen would his outlook on life have undergone a radical change?"*

He was devoted to his father and it would have doubtless caused him great pain and sorrow to differ from him, but he was not afraid of his father in the way that the rest of the family were and it is just possible that he might have escaped the claustrophobic influence of the Benson family household and enabled his brothers and sisters to do likewise. For they remained, as it were, in a magic circle which invisibly enclosed them. Fear of their father, devotion to their mother, even love of the old family nurse, Beth, helped to keep them in a strangely prolonged immaturity. "Our little sheltered boy!" Mrs Benson exclaimed when Hugh, on leaving Eton, wished to

* Henry Sidgwick apologised to Arthur Benson, when the latter left Cambridge, for not having seen more of him. He knew, he said, that the Archbishop was uneasy about his possible influence on Arthur's religious faith and that in consequence he had seen less of his nephew, for whom he had a great affection, than he would have wished.

join the Indian Civil Service,* and that is the keynote
of their parents' attitude. It was not expressed by any
physical restraints; in fact, some of the anecdotes of
their recreations at Lincoln when they used to have
sham fights, besieging an old tower in the garden with
an unguarded flight of stone steps down which they
pushed each other, are hair-raising.† Nor was their
education at all confined or neglected. Not only did
the boys go to public schools and Cambridge, but the
girls were also educated; first at High School at
Truro (founded by the Bishop) and later at Lady
Margaret Hall under Miss Wordsworth, daughter of
the Bishop of Lincoln. But the enclosing influence was
all round them. Arthur, as an undergraduate, was
asked to a supper-party to meet Irving. He happened to
mention this casually to his father who, a few hours later
put into his hand "a long, very affectionate and rather
pathetic letter. He said," Arthur continues, "he would
not think of forbidding me to go, but he spoke of it as if
it were a parting of the ways, and that if I went to such
an entertainment, I might easily be drawn into an
attractive current of the world, with much superficial
charm and interest masking a vague sort of morality and
dubious standards." Arthur refused the invitation.

* He failed the examination and fulfilled his father's dearest
hopes by entering the Anglican Church. Later he managed to
achieve escape from his father's spiritual domination without
forfeiting his need for shelter by entering the protecting arms of
the Roman Catholic Church.

† Martin and Arthur had an even more awful experience in
the cathedral, round which they were allowed to ramble using
their father's pass key. Martin got an attack of vertigo on a
narrow stone walk between the arches eighty feet above the
nave and could neither move backward or forward. He finally
got back holding Arthur's hand.

The girls were even more carefully sheltered. Maggie was not allowed to take part in reading parties at Lady Margaret Hall without a chaperone; nor was she permitted to join a ladies' reading circle since the proposed book was Browning's *A Blot on the Scutcheon*. At twenty-eight, she could write to her mother that she had had for the first time a little taste of the World and the result of it was that she felt: "how enormously and tremendously nicer home is because it hasn't got that element.

> *The world is very evil*
> *The times are waxing late*

is quite what I feel—in the little bit I have had of it—one hears things that make you sick—and I hear remarkably few I know, of what they are."

Arthur Benson described the family as being "rather a close little corporation with clearly defined interests of our own, critical and observant, but not, I trust priggish or superior. Indeed I think we were rather unduly afraid of life, and thought the mêlée a rougher, harsher, less kindly place than it was in reality."

One of the results of this curiously sheltered upbringing was the number of books that they produced. Literature was for them a substitute for life. They all wrote, including the sisters. Nellie, who died before she was thirty, had a novel, some sketches of life among the poor in Lambeth (both published posthumously), and travel notes of a journey to the Holy Land to her credit. Maggie's contributions were more important. Besides a book of animal short stories she spent many years writing and rewriting *The Venture of Rational Faith*, eventually published in 1908. It was an attempt to reconcile the new doctrines of science with the Christian Faith. It has not now been read for many a year and it sheds no new light on the subject but it is logically and lucidly written and it shows an intellectual grasp of which none of her brothers was capable.

It was, however, the three brothers, all best-sellers in their day, who produced the flow of writing whose quantity rather than its quality is so remarkable. All three were compulsive writers in the same sense that certain psychologically disturbed persons are compulsive eaters. It is true that it was their profession and that they lived by their pens. Arthur had been a brilliantly successful housemaster at Eton but he was only too glad to give it up to devote his life to writing; Hugh was granted special permission by his church to forgo pastoral work and to live at Hare Street (which he bought and maintained with his literary earnings), writing and lecturing; Fred, from the very beginning, in spite of his mother's protests, set his face against taking any kind of job but was determined to be a full-time novelist.

The need for money might well explain the enormous quantity they wrote but the true reason lies far deeper than that. They could not stop. To Arthur Benson writing was an absolute drug. He shut himself into his study for three hours every evening between tea and dinner and wrote without ceasing, never erasing, never correcting, throwing the completed sheets into an out-tray whence they were collected and typed by his secretary. Besides his life of his father, he wrote many biographical sketches (which are probably his best works), mostly on contemporary characters, Eton masters, literary confrères and so on. He also wrote novels and poems but his reputation rested upon his books of essays, collections of anodyne great thoughts with such titles as *From a College Window, The Thread of Gold, The Hill of Trouble, Thy Rod and Thy Staff*, and so on. Although he was rather wistful if his friends criticised these works unduly, he did not himself think very highly of them, and would refer to them as "pious varnish" or his "well-known essays which gave such delight in Upper Norwood". Yet in spite of his mock denigration they continued to roll off the end of his pen. Those who cannot face reading them today and yet have a faint curiosity to know what they are like could well content themselves by reading Max Beerbohm's parody in *A Christmas Garland*, which is barely an exaggeration of A. C. Benson's bland style. In addition to all these works and to a voluminous correspondence he kept a diary which runs to four and a half million words. It was edited by Percy Lubbock and extracts from it were published in 1926, but the complete text will not see the light of day before 1975.

Arthur was perhaps the one of the three brothers who was most drugged by the inky marijuana but both Fred and Hugh bear frequent testimony to the spell it laid on them. Both say that they got carried away by their work, that their characters act of their own volition and insist on a life of their own. One can only wonder why, if this is so, their lives are so poor and thin, but perhaps it is something to do with the extraordinary rapidity of their creation. E. F. Benson in particular often wrote the same novel in differing forms. In time he recognised this himself. In *Final*

Edition he describes how he conducted a stocktaking into his own literary past. "I observed with a certain acuteness but not with insight," he wrote. "I made my people bustle about, indulge in what may be called 'stock' experiences, talk with a rather brilliant plausibility, but as a depressed perusal of some of my own volumes convinced me, they lacked the red corpuscle." He also accused himself, truly, of "trying to conceal my own lack of emotion in situations that were intended to be interesting, by daubing them over with sentimentality". This is a depressing but just conclusion. E. F. Benson, if he lives as a writer at all, will depend for his reputation on a few of his horror stories, such as *The Luck of the Vails*,* on his comic sequence of books stemming from Queen Lucia and Miss Mapp, and on his biographies, particularly his volumes of family recollections.

Robert Hugh Benson only wrote less than his brothers because he died earlier. The British Museum lists forty published titles of his as against sixty of Arthur's and over ninety of Fred's.† Like all his family he was passionately interested in his own work. He found his characters "going along quite independently and I can't help it", but his work was marred by its passionate propaganda element. In his historical novels the martyrs are all on one side. In his contemporary ones all the Protestants, particularly the

---

* This rather gruesome little tale was invented by Arthur and told as a serial to the lower boys in his house at Eton. He passed the germ of the story on to Fred. All the Benson brothers had rather a penchant for liking to "make the flesh creep". Robert Hugh Benson's *The Necromancers* is another of this genre.

† This excludes prefaces, edited anthologies, short religious pamphlets, etc.

5b. Edward White Benson, Archbishop of Canterbury

5a. Mrs Benson aet. 19

6b. Nellie and Maggie Benson
at the Chancery, Lincoln

6a. Hugh Benson and 'Beth'
at the Chancery, Lincoln

Anglican vicars, are hidebound, snobbish, reactionary
and hypocritical, while the Catholics are spiritual,
humble-minded and understanding. There are some
rather interesting situations in some of his books: the
young man in *The Coward* who fails in the one quality
that the English upper-class considered absolutely
obligatory; the young man in *An Average Man* who
"had great possessions"; the rather spine-chilling,
spooky atmosphere of *The Necromancers*; but all these
are submerged in the propaganda element and the
flood of somewhat second-rate purplish prose. Moreover, neither he nor his brothers could describe a
credible young woman nor a heterosexual relationship.

Another clue to the curious Benson psychology may
be found in the enormous number of books they wrote
about their past and about themselves as a family.
Arthur, besides the standard *Life of Archbishop Benson*
wrote *The Trefoil*, a book of family reminiscences, a
memoir of his sister Nellie, a life of his sister Maggie
and a life of his brother Hugh.* Fred wrote *Our
Family Affairs*, *Mother*, *As We Were* and *Final Edition*.
Hugh wrote *Confessions of a Convert* which gives, it
must be admitted, a rather inaccurate picture of his
childhood and, like both his brothers, he frequently
introduced real characters into his novels. Benty, the
old nurse in *The Coward*, is an accurate transcription
of Beth. (For a really unkind portrait of an understanding father, modelled partially on the Archbishop,
and a mother who tried to reconcile father and son,

* He also wrote a life of his mother after Mrs Benson's death
in 1918, but although references are made to this work both in
A. C. B.'s *Diary*, edited by Percy Lubbock, and in his unpublished correspondence with Geoffrey Madan, I have been unable to trace a copy.

one should read *Rex* by E. F. Benson.) Their past enchained them. Arthur Benson wrote of a visit to Wellington that he made in 1915. "Every corner was so full of ghosts and memories that I could scarcely get along. I don't want it over again—of that I am certain; but I don't know why it should affect one so powerfully, or what so strong an emotion *means*. Most emotions mean something which is connected with the future, plans or hopes or even fears. But this means nothing but a beautiful sort of past which can't come again, and which I don't *want* to come again. Something strange is hidden behind such a feeling, I believe. But for the life of me I can't see what."

This sense of the past, this continual looking back, was something that all three surviving Benson brothers had in common (Hugh less than the other two) although they had never been very close during their childhood and youth. Age differences precluded this. Arthur was six years older than Fred, ten years older than Hugh. At times he would sweep his juniors into some family ploy such as the founding of a hierarchical chapter of which he was the Grand Master and Hugh was Henchman or general dogsbody. The chapter had minutes, seals and documents but no very clear function. More productive was the *Saturday Magazine*, which was issued irregularly, written on sermon paper and filled without difficulty with every kind of contribution from this family of born pen-pushers. But apart from these collective efforts the brothers went their separate ways. In after life Arthur and Hugh developed a friendship which excluded Fred whom they regarded as a worldly trifler, but except for a general sense of family solidarity and the cement provided by their affectionate sisters they were, in youth, inclined to be critical of each other—an attitude which persisted into mature life.

All three remained keenly aware of each other's idiosyncrasies. "F. [Fred] is insolent and quarrelsome about small things," Arthur wrote, "e.g. he is always questioning statements and proving everyone else to be wrong, but he flies into a terrible passion if the meanest detail of one of his radically inaccurate and even absurd stories is doubted, and says it is the foulest sort of pedantry to be always pulling up a man who just tries to keep things going. F. couldn't be described in a book, because he is such a mass of contradictions. Yesterday he was tremendously cock-a-hoop and walked twenty miles; today he has a touch of neuralgia, and one would suppose it to be cancer from the sombre look of doom on his brow."

Fred, on his side, observed with a keenly analytical insight the strange "double personality" which characterised Arthur. It was, he wrote, "sharply divided, with no connecting point of contact between the two sides of his nature." On one side "he was the most humorous and entertaining of companions, appreciative and incisively critical". The second personality expressed in his books and his replies to his fan mail was "patient, tender, tranquil, following the thread of gold through the crowded labyrinths of life, withdrawn from the crazy tumult and the lure of ambition and effectiveness". He draws a picture of Arthur coming down to breakfast "with upheld hands of horror at the inevitable pile of letters beside his plate", and spending the rest of the morning "under the control of the second personality in writing long and sympathetic answers to the confidences of his admiring readers".

Both elder brothers used to get very irritated with Hugh, who flung himself into verbal conflict with no regard for logic or consistency. This had always been one of his characteristics. "Ride with Hugh," Fred recorded in his diary for 1887 when they both were still schoolboys. "Conversation is difficult . . . argument is impossible chiefly owing to his keenness for his own ideas and consequent blindness to other people's." This trait was in later life naturally reinforced by the combativeness of the convert. Fred records an occasion when "he turned on Aunt Nora Sidgwick,* who with Balfourian calm had pointed out some fatal logical flaw in his argument and said: 'But I belong to a Church which happens to know.'" Nor did he disdain recourse to the lowest of weapons. On another occasion when he maintained that the Papal elections were always directly controlled by the Holy Ghost "he bitterly resented an exasperated brother asking why the Holy Ghost always chose an Italian. 'You hurt me when you say that,' he complained."

Of the three brothers Arthur was the most intellectual and the most interesting. He was an enormous, heavily built man with abundant rough hair and a shaggy moustache. He was well aware of the split in his own personality. "In my books I am solemn, sweet, refined; in real life I am rather vehement, sharp, contemptuous, a busy mocker," he wrote in his diary; and it may have been this curious duality which prevented him from stretching out his hand and taking the

* Nora Balfour, the sister of A. J. Balfour, had married Henry Sidgwick, Mrs Benson's brother.

worldly success which he could have easily have had. For he was extremely able. He had been a most successful housemaster at Eton in spite of his somewhat unconventional methods. Mrs Benson wrote to Maggie that she had met someone from Eton who had told her that "Arthur goes round every night and *tickles* all the boys—and shows them how strong he is —Doesn't it sound funny. Fancy girls!"*

Nevertheless in spite of this eccentricity his house was a good one and he was a good teacher. The third Lord Halifax writes that: "Arthur Benson was the only master who at that time ever made Homer come alive for me, by disposing quite quickly of the 30 lines set for the official lesson and then racing through as much more as the time allowed, so that for half an hour we really caught a little of the romance and poetry of the Greek." Many of Arthur Benson's friends thought that he did his best work as a housemaster and deplored his leaving. He might have succeeded to the Headmastership in place of Doctor Warre and reformed the old dry-as-dust teaching of classics to which Lord Halifax referred. He could not, however, bring himself to stand as a candidate, though Doctor Warre himself implored him to do so and it is almost certain he would have succeeded. He certainly did not want the post but by a curious quirk of character he long bore Eton and his Eton colleagues a grudge because they had not put his name forward without his consent and forced on him a position which he had done everything to avoid. That he was

* Mrs Benson's construction is somewhat elliptical here. Does she mean how odd it would be if Arthur tickled girls or that such goings on would not be tolerated in a girls' school?

sometimes tempted by worldly honours is shown by
his dreams in which he frequently figured, splendidly
dressed, in triumphal processions. (Obviously reminiscences of the Archbishop in cope and mitre swinging
down a cathedral aisle.) But he turned his back on all
these things, just as he turned his back on deeper
emotional fulfilment.

It is possible that a sense of inferiority to Martin
marked Arthur for the rest of his life. All his contemporaries have remarked on the quality of un-
approachability that lay behind the façade of the
genial, warm-hearted conversationalist, companion
and diner-out. It may have stemmed from his childhood, when he was always one step behind Martin. A
brother one and a half years older is unavoidably in a
natural position of superiority but Arthur must have
been aware from a very early age that Martin was
THE one. Arthur got a scholarship at Eton; so did
Martin, but it was thought not good enough for him,
he had to try the higher hurdle of Winchester. Arthur
was gifted and charming, his schoolboy letters to his
mother, often illustrated by little drawings, are delightful. One of them reproaching her for not having
written begins in capital letters:

"GRACELESS MOTHER
WRETCHED REPROBATE,"

Another informs her that he "composed a story yesterday called 'the biology and adventures of a needle'
! ! ! ! ! ! ! ! ! Only Think what an honour to have a
son that is an author!" He was probably more
aesthetic than Martin, with more feeling for music
and art, but these were not the gifts that were prized

in the Benson household. The feeling that it was no use trying to rival Martin, that it was better to lock everything away and not attempt to compete, may account for that lack of nerve, that failure to grasp the nettle, that led him to shun both ambition and emotion. "My own failing," he wrote in his diary, "is that I have never been in vital touch with anyone —never either fought anyone or kissed anyone! Like Dmitri Rudin,* I can neither be soldier or lover— and this not out of any principle, but out of a timid and rather fastidious solitariness."

Nevertheless, he was a splendid companion and a great life enhancer. His friends put up with the iron discipline that he imposed on them (walks and bicycle rides had to be taken at a certain hour, last a certain time and return at a given moment, whatever the weather) because of the lively interest he took in their affairs, because of his geniality and his mordant, dry wit. His talents for describing the *persona* of others are well shown in his most successful works, books of memoirs such as *Memories and Friends* and *The Leaves of the Tree*; but they are even more vividly exercised in his letters and his diary where his waspish tendencies could be given full play—Housman "flicking cold water over any well-meaning efforts to start a talk—his little square mouth and his strangely docked moustache"; Lord Fisher making a public speech: "A naked exhibition of human nature at its lowest closely bordering on the orang outan"; and Lady Mount Temple† "strangely attired—costume de-

* The hero of Turgenev's novel *Rudin* published 1885.
† Lady Mount Temple had been Mrs Cowper Temple, Ruskin's intimate friend and an intermediary in his affair with with Rose La Touche.

signed by Ruskin I expect and with the sort of smile which comes of having been told daily for many years that your smile is like a sunset or a strain of music"— are all characteristic Arthur Benson.

The other two brothers, E. F. and R. H., were lighter weight both metaphorically and literally. E. F. was the one who most nearly succeeded in escaping from the slightly miasmic atmosphere of the family. At the age of twenty-four he thrust an untidy parcel containing an untyped manuscript upon his mother, adjuring her to show it to Henry James and Mrs Harrison, a family friend who, under the name of Lucas Malet, was one of the best-selling novelists of the day, to see if anything could be done about it. The young author used to reflect in after years with ruefulness but also with some amusement on Henry James's probable reactions on receiving this hastily written, blotted manuscript, so alien to all his own standards of care and precision. He was as usual courteous and wrote to the young author saying that perhaps he was not a fair judge as he was obsessed by form and style in novels and as he put it: "I am not sure that yours strikes me as so ferociously literary as my ideal." Lucas Malet was more helpful. She proffered some valuable advice as to rewriting and recommended a publisher who accepted it immediately. Fred was in Greece on an archaeological dig at the time and when he returned in the spring of 1894 the book, entitled *Dodo*, was published. It was the story of a "modern girl", a young, hard, vital creature, who flirted and smoked and talked nonsense, flouting both the current *mores* of society and the sentimental convictions of her elders. She was generally supposed to be a portrait of

Margot Tennant. The book caught on and Fred "awoke to find himself famous". A personable young man, a mild celebrity, the son of an Archbishop, who is amusing, intelligent and good at golf and bridge, will never find himself at a loss for invitations, and from that moment Fred escaped into the great world. He golfed at Overstrand with the Batterseas, went to Bayreuth with the Charles Beresfords and attended the great weekend parties given at Cliveden by Lady de Grey. Judging by his books there may have been some inner conflict in his rejection of his family standards and the adoption of those of the smart set. At one period he wrote several novels (*Rex*, *Peter*, etc.), about a smooth, successful young man who makes himself universally pleasant and has a reputation for kindness and unselfishness which masks a heart as hard as a stone. The same theme is repeated, translated into a feminine key, in *The Climber*, probably his best novel, which deals with a poor, beautiful girl, who ruthlessly snatches a rich and priggish peer from her best friend. Her selfish heartlessness, accompanied as it is by tremendous *joie de vivre* and delight in worldly pleasures is very well described. Something of the same theme is also explored in a singularly bad book called *Colin* about a young man whose ancestor has sold his soul to the devil in return for grandeur and riches and who implicitly makes the same bargain. There is, however, little to be gained by trying to dissect a novelist's life from his works and if E. F. Benson did have a period during which he found the simple evangelical standards in which he had been brought up both boring and narrow and yet could not quite adapt himself to the current cynicism of society, this is

pure conjecture. One thing is certain, he was always the
one who was left to deal with the practical problems
facing the family. It was he who consoled his mother in
the early days of her widowhood; who signed the paper
committing Maggie to the asylum and was her most
regular visitor throughout her illness. Although it was
Arthur who was summoned to Hugh's deathbed, Fred
had the business of going down to Hare Street and
arranging for the disposal of Hugh's effects; he had
the same melancholy task to perform after his mother's
death at Tremans and finally, the last living member
of the family, he disposed of the enormous jumble of
Arthur's possessions at Magdalene in 1925.

The third brother, Robert Hugh, was in some
respects the most peculiar of the three. He was a
strange little boy. He was described by his family as
looking "rather angelic" but in his photographs he
gives more the impression of a goblin child. The things
that the family were unitedly agreed upon were that
he was quite uninfluenceable both in conduct and in
argument, and that he was strangely detached from
his fellow creatures. "The most remarkable thing
about him," Arthur wrote, "was a real independence
of character, with an entire disregard of other people's
opinion. What he liked, what he felt, what he decided
was the important thing to him and so long as he
could get his way, I do not think that he troubled his
head about what other people might think or wish;
he did not want to earn good opinions, nor did he
care for disapproval or approval; people were in fact
to him at the time just more or less favourable channels for him to follow his own designs, more or less
stubborn obstacles to his attaining his wishes."

If this picture is accurate, and it is borne out by other quotations from Fred and Maggie, it seems that Hugh was abnormally self-centred. Psychologists may like to take into account the fact that his mother was very ill after his birth and that during his first year of life she was away at Wiesbaden. Yet he was not a child deprived of love. Beth, the family nurse, who had brought up not only the little Bensons but their mother and uncles, showed him unstinting devotion. "We were all her children," wrote Fred, "and the darlingest of all to Beth's big heart was Hugh." Once the family was established at Truro Mrs Benson gave him his lessons as she had once taught Martin and Arthur and was continually writing to his godmother, Susan Wordsworth, detailing his progress, his quickness and his charms; while he was the apple of his father's eye. "I am surprised at the intelligent interest Hugh takes in it," (the 1st Epistle of St John), the Archbishop wrote in his diary in July, 1883. "God favour the boy. He is very like Martin only less delicate looking. This boy is the picture of ruddy force; light and strong."

Yet in spite of all this outpouring of love and attention or just possibly because of it, Hugh continued to take his own way, self-contained, uninfluenceable, the cat that walks by itself.

∘ VI ∘

Mrs Benson was unlike most mothers in that she preferred her daughters to her sons. All her children adored her and she was devoted to them all, giving them unstintingly of her time, her advice, her company but she could view her boys briskly and with detachment. She could write of Arthur's "swift, furious, baseless" moods; of Hugh as being "too foolish", and of Fred's mind as "so inaccurate that his absolute certainty . . . goes for very little". Nor was she much impressed by their literary work. "I was going swimmingly along," she wrote of *Mammon & Co.* by E. F. Benson, "when suddenly a thumping irresponsible incident (of the usual worst order) cuts clear across all the weavings of character and is followed by equally impossible mawkish sentimental Christian forgiveness. . . . His knowledge of human nature with regard to mother and babies is as incomplete as you might expect." There is a delightful incident recorded in *Final Edition* of all three brothers spending the afternoon writing parodies of each other's books. Arthur, who had closeted himself with *The Light Invisible* by Hugh, led off with a study of "an aged and saintly Roman Catholic priest" who, while doddering about his garden "had seen a woman dressed in a blue robe with stars in her hair standing by a bush of rosemary. She smiled and vanished so it was not difficult to guess who *she* was. . . ." Fred wrote about a "wise patient wistful middle-aged gentleman called Geoffrey, who sate* by his mullioned window and looked out on the gracious flowing meadow below, where a stream ran between banks of feathery grass and willow-herb and loosestrife". Hugh took Fred for his model and E. F. professed to feel that the presentation of "those bubbling puppets with their inane, inconsequent talk" missed its mark. "But here was my mother for the third time wiping tears of joy from her eyes, and Arthur and, of course, the author were much amused.

" 'Oh, you clever people!' said my mother. 'Why don't you all for the future write each other's books instead of your own? You do them much better.' "

The relationship between Mrs Benson and her daughters differed in quality from that between her and her sons. She writes of the "awful inner tie between mother and daughter" and there is no doubt that she was closer to Maggie, at least, than to any of her other children. The affection was returned in almost too full measure: "Mother," Maggie wrote in 1885, "do you know the thought of you makes me feel the existence of an active and powerful principle of good in the world and in people. I mean you seem to illuminate things for me somehow."

The two sisters (there was only a year between them) were to some degree the focus of the whole family. In early days they formed a link between the two worlds of the godlike schoolboys, Martin and Arthur, and the nursery life of Fred and Hugh. In after years Arthur had set out on his own career before his brothers had reached public school age, while Fred and Hugh who had four years between them were never very congenial. But the sisters, in the middle of the family,

* Arthur always used this tiresome archaism.

reached both upwards and downwards and their letters to their brothers at school are charmingly affectionate and give delightful pictures of Victorian family life.

Nellie, the elder of the two, most resembled her mother both physically and in character. She was rather fat and square and she had an extrovert sunny nature, a desire to please and to make friends. She possessed a natural gaiety though she was at times overshadowed by the dark neurasthenic melancholy which was the family curse. She realised, she wrote, that "in one sense" her moods arose from physical causes—(she suffered a great deal from rheumatism) —but, she went on, "this fact remains . . . that the remorse and the despair and the various other noxious component parts of them do, though out of proportion, fix upon the really weak points".

She put, however, a very brave face on these moments of weakness and despair. "There was a mood, Arthur wrote, "in which she tended to stare fixedly before her, and to enliven proceedings with a doleful little song. But she hid her tiredness very gallantly, and it was little suspected. It was a happy temperament full of curiosity and liveliness; and I never saw anyone who was more fitted by nature to be a wife and the happy mother of children." However that may be, in actual fact Nellie seems once again to have resembled her mother in that her emotional contacts, as far as can be judged by her surviving correspondence, were centred on those of her own sex. This was in part due to the excessive prolongation of childhood which was common to all Victorians but particularly marked as we have seen in the Benson family. The ups and downs of friendships and the sentimental relationships which took place at Lady Margaret Hall would nowadays be more usual in schoolgirls of thirteen or fourteen. Nellie kept many packets of letters with instructions that they were to be burnt at her death but one, from a contemporary called Ethel Matthews, for some reason escaped. Ethel, who was a dreary girl, alternates between rejoicing in their friendship: "It seems too great a happiness to think that you care for me so much", and adolescent reproaches. "I told you," she wrote, "my very inmost secret trouble . . . and begged your sympathy and advice. And you took not the slightest notice. I cannot understand how you or anyone *could* leave such a letter unanswered." And again, "You asked to ask me to walk, drive or sit with you almost every day. Only twice this term have you asked me to come with you." All this is pure schoolgirl stuff but there is obviously more reality in Nellie's later relationship with Ethel Smyth, the composer.

Ethel Smyth's first contact with the family came through Mrs Benson. The latter rather fancied herself as a *Directrice des Ames* and Ethel Smyth was confided to her as a patient by Mrs Mandell Creighton, the wife of the historian who was later Bishop of London. It is unnecessary to go into the stormy complications of Miss Smyth's love life which led to her needing a prop; it is sufficient to say that she herself recorded that "from 1886 onwards the mainstay of my life had been Mrs Benson". Ethel Smyth soon became a family friend (although her relationship with the Archbishop of whom she stood "in deadlier awe than of anyone I ever met", was not a happy one). Of the boys she knew Fred best—he puts her into *Dodo* as "Edith Staines"—but the one of the younger generation who, she wrote, "eventually became my particular friend" was Nellie. This is a staid way of putting it. The depth of their relationship and the way it affected Mrs Benson is shown by what one cannot help regarding as a most peculiar letter written by the latter in October 1889 to Ethel Smyth. "Think over the past—we meet first you and I—we sound depths together—and out of that there grows a relation—a deep relation. (Perhaps these last two months may have revealed to me more of the depth of this relation on my part than I quite knew.) This goes on. I know, I know, though you may think I don't what a full and generous gift you pour on me— Ah my child, you have never half believed how I have known this or how sacredly I have reverenced and loved it. But I am slow—and I grieve. Then there comes this new drawing together of you and Nellie—I don't understand it just at first . . . all this means on either side. But it soon dawns on me. You speak of 'confession and wear and tear on all sides'—and by Allah, it *comes*. *But*—and here we come to our present crux, your way out of it I cannot make mine. The play of nature between Nellie and me—the awful inner tie of mother and daughter and, if you will, *my own limitations* speak all together in clear tones and a most deep inner instinct bids me be still, bids *me*, so to speak, 'get out of the way'—while this relation which is evidently increasing more than either of you knew it would, develops itself."

One cannot wholly elucidate this letter, but what does strike one about the Victorians is the extraordinary depth of emotional feeling and of strangely unconventional emotional relationships that lay beneath the conventional, ordinary, day-to-day behaviour.

7. The Benson Family at Truro, Cornwall
Left to right: Nellie, Mrs Benson, Bishop Benson,
Arthur, Maggie
In front: 'Watch' the collie, Hugh, Fred

8. Mrs Benson and her sons.
Left to right: Fred, Hugh, Arthur

Nellie died suddenly and unexpectedly of diphtheria a year after this letter was written and her passing left a great gap in the family circle. The Christmas play was discontinued; the family magazine, produced at intervals since their earliest childhood, was abandoned; the corporate family life lost its gaiety and its spirit. Nellie was, after Martin's death, of all his children, the one who had been least afraid of her father and she had had a close and special relationship with two of her brothers (no-one got very close to Hugh), but the person who probably missed her most was her sister. There was only a year between them and they had done everything together. Moreover, Nellie had shielded her younger sister from many of the jars and difficulties of life in the Benson household. Nellie had a social and outgoing nature and was intensely interested in her fellow creatures. She was thus able to take the lead and prepare the way for her younger sister. Maggie was extremely shy and, like her father, unduly sensitive to all shades of human feeling, but she had been able to make social contacts under her sister's wing. She had now to take up the burden for herself. Arthur Benson describes her at Nellie's funeral as "pale and smiling through her tears, and," he continued, "I was conscious that there was a great tenderness about her, as if she had vowed herself to fill as far as possible, Nellie's place as daughter and sister."

Too much was asked of daughters in Victorian days. When the move was made from Truro to Lambeth Nellie was recalled from Lady Margaret Hall, since it was felt there must be a daughter at home. It may have been reasonable since her health at Oxford had not been good, but one wonders if she had any say in the matter. The tiresome Ethel Matthews wrote exhorting her to contentment: "It appears to me that the ideal life of a daughter at home is to be always at the beck and call of all one's people and even to be doing things for them before they call . . . only having work of one's own to fill up spare moments." Nellie may not have acquiesced in this dreary picture of the ideal (in another letter Miss Matthews says that she knows Nellie could have chosen almost any other life than her own) but she soon found her niche at Lambeth. She was passionately interested in social work and besides being "always at the beck and call" of her people, she ran Girls' Clubs, Sunday Schools and Boys' Evening Classes. Herein she found her fulfilment but Maggie, who succeeded her at Oxford, was cut out for the scholastic life. She took to it like a duck to water. "My work is awfully nice this term," she wrote to her mother "I have political economy twice a week . . . I have moral philosophy with a very good person indeed, a pupil of Green of the *Prolegomena*. He gives me awful essays to do at present—the relation of Moral Philosophy to practice. Then I go to Political Science lectures and write papers for them, and go to another course at the Schools. Altogether it is most delightful. It is so nice getting back to work again—especially such inspiring work as the Moral Philosophy." She was not at all overburdened by her work, however. The other sides of her nature had full play. Her painting came on enormously and Ruskin, watching her copy a painting by him of a purple and white snail shell, told her that he could teach her nothing further, while the emotional side of her nature found its outlet in a large number of very close friendships.

She left Oxford in a blaze of glory with a First in the Women's Honour School of Philosophy. Her coach, a tutor at Keble, wrote: "That wretched 'Women's' Examination: if it had only been Greats! No-one will realise how brilliantly she has done."

The four years between the time that she came down from Oxford and Nellie's death in 1890 were perhaps the happiest in Maggie Benson's life. She was part of the family circle, she had this extra close tie with her mother, she studied, wrote, painted, stayed with her Oxford friends and was prevented from too much introspection by Nellie's cheerful humour and common sense. After Nellie's death, however, her own intense nature came under too great a strain. "Her friendships," Arthur Benson wrote, "were seldom leisurely or refreshing things. . . . Then too, when she was at home, she threw herself into social duties, and her shyness, which was still there though not superficially visible, made the smallest occasion into something of an effort. . . . She never learnt the trick of easy prattle; conversation with her meant thought and feeling and sympathy."

Maggie took the classic Victorian way of escaping from this strain. She retreated into ill-health. It began with rheumatism and a threatening of arthritis. Her heart was affected and there followed a serious illness which attacked both throat and eyes. From 1890 to 1896 she led a more or less invalid life and was forced to spend her winters abroad in a warm climate.

In 1893 she joined Fred who was excavating in Athens and from there they went on to Egypt. It was there that she first began to show some signs that she might like to break away from the sheltering wings that had hitherto enveloped her. She wrote to her mother that she felt that, "for the first time almost", she had had "a little taste of the world at Athens". "In one's life at home," she continued, "one really isn't much thrown across people who have other standards and beliefs. And oh, I do like my native kind so much the best—as I do care so much more for green fields and grey skies than for palm trees and deserts and temples."

Nevertheless it is plain from her letters that the palm trees exercised a certain fascination. She is careful to explain to her mother that she doesn't want to see any more of the World, that 'home' is far nicer and better, but she adds: "The only thing I should like more of—it will amuse you but I feel quite capable of saying it out loud—is the society of young men. I have had much more of that than of girls since I came out— naturally with Fred." Even after Fred left her she still managed to have "furious conversation" with the two men left at the *table d'hôte* of the hotel; discussions on friendship, the value of life, the basis of religion, falling in love at first sight and all the usual weighty topics that young people continually mull over from generation to generation. She contemplated asking one of them to come to Lambeth in the summer and added that he had invited her to see Ibsen's *Master Builder* but somehow things seem to have gone wrong. "One of my little friends has gone," she wrote. "He was so amiable when I had a cold, as to send in a book (he had previously lent me one of Meredith's) in case, if I was unwell, that I should find Meredith too stiff. . . . The other man is getting a little bored and boring, he asked me to come out for a sail with him however the other day, but fortunately there was an excuse ready."

THE BENSONS

Maggie Benson was much prettier than Nellie; she was tall and slender with an air of distinction, and had given up the habit of parting her hair in the middle and plastering it down on either temple. Nevertheless she must have been a rather daunting prospect for any young man. Her first-class brain with its lucidity of thought and dry reasonableness, combined with her intense nature and sheltered upbringing, were in a way formidable. Whether she herself, unlike Miss Buss and Miss Beale, was ever touched by 'Cupid's dart' is not clear. In the winter of 1895-6, when she was again at Luxor, allowed (in what seems nowadays a curiously haphazard way) to undertake excavations at the Temple of Karnak, her predilections seem to have run more on the lines of those observable in her mother and sister, for her letters are full of one Nettie Gourlay. Nettie was rather a plain, abnormally silent young woman of thirty-three, but Maggie found in her more than met the ordinary eye. "Oh Mother," she wrote, "it's so odd to me to make a friendship like this— generally there has been something in the way— mostly I've not been sure of the other person and generally I've had a radical element of distrust. But here one can't help trusting her *absolutely*, and it's only myself I distrust. She is so much bigger, and so much finer and more delicate in mind than most women."

Nettie remained Maggie Benson's intimate friend and close companion, tolerated rather than loved, one feels, by the rest of the Benson family. There are a few clues, however, to show that Maggie might perhaps, had things gone well, have rejoiced in a more normal relationship. Arthur Benson in his life of his sister simply says that "at this time" [1890-6] "she passed through a particular emotional crisis, which affected her whole life deeply and left its mark on her". During much of this period various allusions are made in the correspondence between mother and daughter to one"L. J." who was one of the Archbishop's chaplains. Mrs Benson is inclined rather to laugh at him (he seems to have been a somewhat serious young man) but Maggie obviously felt differently because in her diary for September 28th, 1896, when she was touring with the Archbishop in Ireland, Mrs Benson wrote:

"I got L. J.'s letter *it destroyed me*. I found Maggie's letter which was just *all*. Generosity and Liberty breathed thro' it—there was no bitterness and no death." Another entry for October 5th elucidates the matter: "L. J. to Maggie showing clearly that he had cared for Miss Trefusis for 10 years. Well, well, it will hurt I know—but God can heal."

○ VII ○

The ten years of Archbishop Benson's Primacy (1886-1896) were perhaps the happiest in Mary Benson's married life. She enjoyed the bustle and stir of the great world. Although not a worldly woman she, quite naturally, also enjoyed their position of importance, of feeling at the centre of things and the multitude of people who flowed through Lambeth Palace. "We had a Queen at our last garden-party we had," Maggie wrote to her brother Hugh in 1888, "and as Mar and Par were both ordered down to Windsor to dine with the other Queen (of England I mean)—we are so sought after by the Royal Family—Nellie and I had to entertain the first Queen, who was from Hawaii. She had an interpreter, who told her Wiclif was the first Archbishop—and stopped her by a nod when she wanted to put her sponge cake in her tea."

Mrs Benson never seems to have been troubled or worried by the difficulties of running two large households (Lambeth and Addington Park, at that time the country residence of the Archbishops of Canterbury). There were excellent and devoted servants and the old troubles at Wellington over bills and money seem to have completely subsided. Archbishop Benson grumbled about too much social life, about entertaining and being entertained, but appeared to enjoy it very much when it was in process. In any case a great deal of it was necessary in his position. "Life is roaring on," Mrs Benson wrote to Maggie in 1893.

"Dinner of 30 Sat. 55 Junior Clergy yesterday. 40 Bps. tonight."

Her children were all at home in the holidays, they and their friends flashing in and out of the house, riding, skating, getting up plays. She had a devoted circle of female friends who were privileged to call her Ben, among whom was Lucy Tait, the daughter of the last Archbishop, who had come to live with the Bensons after Nellie's death. Her husband was more and more dependent on her in every way and it seemed that her one desire in life was to do him service.

Nevertheless, all was not entirely well. Edward Benson was still subject to those terrible black moods of depression which had pursued him all his life. They were not so bad as they had been once and she was even able to laugh at him gently though not perhaps to his face. "The hot-house heat," she wrote to Maggie, "takes the starch out of all except your father whom it stimulates to abnormal criticism of the world around and reflections on how he is letting the position down." Yet in spite of her sense of proportion these neurasthenic depressions took their toll more of her than of him. E. F. Benson writes of them as follows: "Then, more completely than ever, but with some sort of enslavement she was his, for her anxiety and fear chained her to him in his dark places not for his enlightenment, but for her eclipse." She suffered from an unanalysable dread, which would centre itself on recognisable objects such as her husband's health or her children's safety (she could not bear to watch them start off when they were riding) but was really an undefined sense of panic. This enemy was continually attacking her and forbidding her to sleep. "This has been a dreadful time," she wrote on September 28th, 1896, "my own shrinking from the nights has been terrible to me."

Another symptom of chronic unease was her difficulty in keeping her weight down. E. F. Benson takes this very lightly: "She deliciously records in her diary the rules she made for herself and quite as deliciously the breaking of them," but with our modern knowledge of compulsive eating it is quite plain that all these entries: "I am going to be *perfectly firm* till midday of the 16th and take my weight then"; "Scarcely any loss of weight I *am* going to be rigid this week", show a disturbed psyche.

It might be argued that this excess of fear was purely rational. The Archbishop had a heart condition and was never a man to spare himself. Yet the doctors were completely reassuring and made no effort to stop the official visit he was about to make to Ireland. It was during this visit that the diary rises to a crescendo of panic and the news about Maggie and L. J. added to the writer's sense of misery. Yet the tour was a great success; the Archbishop seemed to enjoy every moment of it and when, at its finish, they arrived to spend the weekend at Hawarden, sat up late at night in vigorous conversation with Mr Gladstone.

The next morning the whole party attended Morning Service. During the Confession the Archbishop's head fell forward and he was heard to breathe rather stertorously. He was lifted up and carried out but before they could bring him to the house he was dead. Those who were of his intimate circle felt, as Hugh Benson put it, "as if the roof were gone".

The greatest shock was of course sustained by Mrs

Benson. Her life had become, she wrote, like a string of beads when the thread is cut. Yet even at this moment she did not pretend that things had been otherwise than they were; she never minimised the wrong he had done her. He had chosen her freely but she had been forced into her response. It was not, she felt, till she knelt beside his body covered with the white pall in Canterbury Cathedral that she chose him "with a full heart". "O Edward," she wrote, three months after his death, "is it possible that now, in the bosom of God you see all the past and understand that I did not choose before? and that you are *wanting* me to choose you—and choosing me afresh—I must have been a bitter disappointment that is over. You won't mind waiting in the Home of Love and I must get myself first."

The same string was still being plucked three months later. "I realise that he chose me deliberately," she wrote, "as a child who was very fond of him and whom he might educate—he even wanted to preserve himself from errant fallings in love. . . . And the strain and pressure from that time till now was such that every interval was to me a kind of holiday in which I drew breath and played."

Yet now that "the strain and pressure", which had endured for forty-three years, were lifted she could not at first feel any sense of relief—only a terrible sense of loss and a feeling that no-one wanted her. "*I was not associated with him in people's minds*," she wrote in her diary a year and a half after the Archbishop's death. "*His* friends did not and do not seek me. . . . And yet I toiled to make myself agreeable to his friends. No, they did not want my 2d. agreeableness—they wanted his massiveness, his large ideas, his power. *And I was never associated with these. . . .* What can I do now? at 57 not very vigorous—having spent all my life in scrappy interruptions—small means—fat and ugly."

Poor Mrs Benson's search for rest and refreshment and a viable way of life was further complicated by the problem of Maggie. She was perhaps the most dearly loved of all the children, "the child of her heart" as Fred puts it, and the six years of bad health during which her mother had smoothed her every path and cherished her had added to the devotion on both sides. "*O* Maggie and O Maggie I *do* want you so," Mrs Benson wrote in 1893, "I just want you home to look in your dear face and *have you* and all will follow as it should." Yet after her father's death an extraordinary change began to take place in Maggie.

The winter of 1896-7 was spent by the Benson family in Egypt. This was, of course, conceived as a recuperative measure, but it proved the very opposite, for Maggie almost died of a heart attack and both Fred and Lucy Tait succumbed to typhoid fever. Battered and weary the convalescent family returned to England and endeavoured to cram the contents of Lambeth and Addington, including a small billiard table, a two-manual organ, several sets of the *Early Christian Fathers* and a seated and life-size statue of Rameses the Great, into a pleasant early-Georgian house in Winchester. The permanent household was to consist of Mrs Benson, Fred, Maggie and Lucy Tait.

It is difficult to form any impression of Lucy Tait, for very little has been written about her. She was a large woman, she must have towered over the diminutive Minnie Benson, she was much given to good works and she was soaked in the atmosphere of the Anglican Church.* She was the daughter of Archbishop Tait, Benson's predecessor, and as a baby she had survived the cataclysmic onslaught of scarlet fever during which her parents had lost five daughters between ten and two years of age. After Nellie's death she had come to live with the Bensons as a sort of supplementary daughter, being half-way in age between Mrs Benson and Maggie. The Archbishop was very fond of her. "Meggie [his usual version of his daughter's name] and Lucy are delightful companions," he wrote in his diary, and again: "Lucy Tait, who not only thinks how she may serve her friends but if there is one way more thorough than another does it, goes out with Meggie to Caux". Maggie at this time also seems to have accepted her though she was perhaps a little scornful of Lucy's intellectual capabilities,† but it was Mrs Benson who relied on Lucy, leaned on her and requited her with more than ordinary affection. E. F. Benson writes that "it was impossible to think of them apart" and he also adds the information that cannot help filling us with a faint distaste that: "Lucy slept with

* She once complained that Mrs Benson had no sympathy with the poor, only with culture, and that she put the convenience of her family above the good of others.

† "A discussion has been raging downstairs about Deceased Wife's Sister—and such-like things," she wrote to Nettie Gourlay in 1896. "Lucy's position is grand.
  (1) The laity needn't give way to the clergy because they constitute the Church as much as the clergy do.
  (2) The clergy must give way to the laity because otherwise there would be a split.
The reason why the clergy must give way, and not the laity, is because the laity have more commonsense."
Such pragmatic thinking did not commend itself to one who might have taken a First in Greats.

my mother in the vast Victorian bed where her six
children had been born in Wellington days".

Cooped up in the small Winchester house, Maggie
began to be jealous of Lucy Tait. She saw her as
assuming her place as daughter of the house and in Mrs
Benson's heart. This was perhaps intelligible but
another change was taking place in Maggie's nature
which made life extremely difficult. She had never
been on easy terms with her father. Nellie, who was
not afraid of him, had got on with him far better.
Maggie and the Archbishop were too alike, too thin-
skinned, too conscious of another's disapproval to live
on a comfortable basis. They were fond of each other,
proud of each other, but between them there was a
sense of strain. After his death, however, she began
what can only be called 'a cult' for him. She was
editing an unpublished treatise by him entitled *Revela-
tion* and some addresses delivered at Lambeth. She was
also helping Arthur with the official *Life*. Mrs Benson
was much in favour of this. Her letters show how much
more she esteemed Maggie's intellectual capacity than
Arthur's. "O Maggie," she wrote, "Arthur on the Box
seat—don't get over-done—I am so transcendantly
happy that your hand is on it now," and in a letter to
Hugh she wrote: "A great step has been made, Arthur
has turned over to Maggie a great part of the Life—
the chapters on the Ecclesiastical matters . . . and I do
think it will come out all right". The result, however,
of all this soaking in her father's work was that "his
very personality, dominating and masterful, and his
sense of responsibility for the spiritual strenuousness of
those round him began to take possession of her.
Hitherto," E. F. Benson continues, "such traits had

been non-existent in her, she had been indulgent and genial, leaving others to pursue their own paths, and never desirous of bending them to her own angle."

This severity of judgment was accompanied by some of the black gloom that used to envelop the Archbishop. How much distress this metamorphosis caused her mother is shown by the following extracts from the latter's diary for 1898.

Maggie plunged in deep gloom . . . a good deal due to liver conditions but the old suspicious element came in. . . . I thought that this time I wd. try if we couldn't meet the attack cheerfully I mean on my side—I set before me this plan: To give no ground of offence by anything— not to be betrayed into a cross word . . . and to try and steady her conditions with my mind instead of feeling them with my nerves and heart.

This plan does not seem to have worked successfully for a later entry reads: "M. and I had driven with Beth to North End. O what a drive! she scarcely spoke and was most curt—I tried many subjects . . . one was I asked her whether she was interested in Church Reform. 'No,' she said, 'I'm not' so that ended it."

Maggie continued to have these depressions and Mrs Benson found herself reliving some of the worst moments of her married life. "What am I to do?" she asked herself. "Am I really very selfish? . . . And yet I feel it wd. be very bad for her if I had no life of my own, but lived only for *her*. There is in her displeasure, as there was in her father's, a power of bringing one into bondage—a dreadful fear . . . in a horrid *relative* self-conscious way that I catch myself acting as of old in a sort of dull slave spirit."

Maggie seems to have inherited the Archbishop's power of keeping everyone around him walking on egg-shells. Mrs Benson wrote that she found herself not showing Maggie a letter from the Bishop of Natal because she was not mentioned in it; that she was glad not to be going to stay with Hugh since Maggie might not like it and that there stretched before her "a long vista of slavery *never* knowing what she (Maggie) would like, avoiding too much companionship with Lucy".

It is probable that, since Maggie's depressions were psychotic, if she had not had a grievance ready to her hand in the presence of Lucy Tait, she might well have picked on some other complaint as a source of friction. It is, however, only too plain that her jealousy of Lucy was deeply fixed and rooted. It was partly the jealousy of a daughter seeing her place usurped, but in her new-found identification with her father she may also have felt something of a husband's resentment. Mrs Benson records: "A terrible talk . . . with Maggie. . . . We entered into a long discussion of what I called her spirit of judging. . . . We got near a most difficult point —the likeness in some ways to her father that was coming out in her, partly through circumstances, partly through her soaking herself in him and his life and thought (really falling in love with her father). She dwelt, with great care on Lucy's influence on me being with me *day* and *night** . . . and that she and I had been growing apart. Her gist was that she felt the growing apartness, and, apparently, the difference in my relation to Lucy now, and three years ago."

Though Mrs Benson was prepared to give up much for Maggie she was not prepared to sacrifice Lucy.

* Mrs Benson underlined these words.

The latter seems to have stood almost in the place of a second husband. What the relationship was exactly we shall never know but it certainly transcended mere friendship as the following extracts from Mrs Benson's diary show: "Once more and with shame O Lord grant that all carnal affections may die in me, and that all things belonging to the spirit may live and grow in me. Lord look down on Lucy and me, and bring to pass the union we have both so blindly, each in our own region of mistake, continually desired."

And again: "It still remains as it ever did for her to be strong and continuous in spirit, for me to be yielding and dependent, not with the dependence of fear, which I tend to have too much, but of love inspiring my living spirit as well as hers."

One thing could be done for Maggie's sake, and that was to move from Winchester. The summer of 1898 had been very hot and she had taken a great dislike to the airless hollow in which Winchester lies, to the narrow garden which walled her in. With her new-found likeness to the Archbishop she had also developed another of his traits, his love of organising and of shouldering responsibilities. Her health prevented her from doing much or from going far afield, so it was decided that a small country estate where she could supervise pigs, poultry and flower-beds would best suit her. "In the country she can have a sphere," her mother told Fred. "Something to look after. A sphere." Mrs Benson herself had no particular love for Winchester; she regretted, naturally enough, the delights of her past life. "I am utterly ashamed at the large place which the luxuries and excitements and position and varieties of Lambeth hold in my sense of loss"—

but she had no desire to bury herself in even deeper country. However, if it was needful for Maggie's sake it would be done, and in the spring of 1899 the whole party, including the dog, the cat, the parrots, the manual hand organ, the statue of Rameses, the Archbishop's folios and everything else was transferred from Winchester to a small country estate called Tremans, near Horsted Keynes in Sussex, where it remained, depleted only by death, till Mrs Benson herself died in 1918.

Tremans is a delightful, rambling house, the oldest part of which was built in the sixteenth century by a kinsman of Thomas Wyatt the poet. The main part of the house is of red brick of the time of Charles II and it has a garden on different levels descending to a small stream. It was a fortunate and happy choice, although the immediate results of the move were not ameliorative; Maggie and her mother were both far too prone to seize "that fatal knife, Deep questioning, which probes to endless dole." As late as 1902 Mrs Benson was still writing letters like the following: "My dear & Precious Person . . . I feel as if you were wandering further and further in some strange region and my voice can't reach you. But it SHALL. It seems as if you were following a mirage and I love far too well not to try and tear you back. . . . *You know in your soul that you have been mistaken in your idea of me.* . . . You have before you a principle that you won't and don't judge. But in actual practice I never knew anyone judge more rapidly, promptly and without appeal."

Nevertheless for a time the shadows did withdraw. Maggie finished her work on her father's books and his censorious spirit retreated from her. She did, as her mother had hoped, find 'a sphere' in organising the garden, the bantams, the peacocks, etc. She started to rewrite her own book, *The Venture of Rational Faith*. She made another great friend, Gladys Bevan, and with her organised a society called the 'St Paul's Association of Rational Study.' Arthur Benson describes these eight years at Tremans as the happiest of her life.

Meanwhile there were other problems for Mrs Benson. Fred, after his father's death, had promised to live with his mother and had been delighted with the house at Winchester. Life in a small provincial town was, as he afterwards demonstrated at Rye,* exactly to his taste. Tremans, in what was then completely rural country, eight miles from the nearest golf course, did not suit him at all and he sulked to such an extent that Mrs Benson was forced to write him "an exhaustive letter setting him free, body and spirit and financially".†
E. F. Benson treated this episode three times; once, fictionally, in *Rex*, once in *Mother* and once in *Final Edition*. In *Mother* he says that she wrote him "the perfect pearl of a letter" and expatiates on this, but in *Final Edition* he says that "elsewhere" he had treated the situation with a "fictitious sentimentality" and that "in this transaction there was really not a touch of it". So Fred took a flat in London and started his career as a professional writer and a man-about-town. His mother did not much approve of either incarnation; she had hoped that his severance from Tremans would drive him to look for work and she had little sympathy

* E. F. Benson took Lamb House after Henry James's death in 1916 and lived there on and off till he himself died in 1940.

† It is not clear whether she simply forwent his contribution to household expenses or made him an allowance till he could find his feet.

with his social pretensions. "His manservant sticks in my throat," she wrote, "it now appears he is going to take him abt. to places, and bring *him here* and I squirm a little at that tho' of course I have not said a single word. A strong young man, with all his income to make should scarcely go about with a man do you think." Nevertheless he was well and happy and once he was no longer bound to Tremans he came down frequently as a guest and became very fond of it.

Hugh presented the next problem to his mother, for he was plainly rushing into the arms of the Roman Catholic Church. Had the Archbishop still been living there would have been much more *Stürm und Drang*, for in spite of his love of ceremony and ritual Edward White Benson set his face sternly against Rome. As a schoolboy he had gone to hear Newman preach and though captivated by the eloquence and the sweet voice he recoiled in horror from what he described as: "the terrible lines deeply ploughed all over his face and the craft that sat upon his retreating forehead and sunken eyes". Benson's prejudices were by no means abated in later life. "It is not too much to say," wrote Arthur Benson,* "that from boyhood there had been steadily growing up in him a deep antagonism both to the errors of doctrine and to the arrogant claims of Rome. . . . To render to the Virgin any part of the homage, to the Church any part of the trust due to their Lord, struck him with a peculiar horror . . . in later life . . . he sometimes exclaimed with a hushed vehemence that he could almost believe that Rome was Antichrist." What he would have said, what he

* Or possibly Maggie, since she was responsible for the Church chapters in her father's life.

would have felt could he have known that his Benjamin, his substitute for Martin, was to become part of that Antichrist, one can only speculate. It is possible that Hugh himself was impelled in this direction by unconscious opposition to his father. His spirit was deeply alien to the imposition of another's personality, and it may be that in the Church of Rome he found both the shelter and the security that all the Bensons seemed to need and also an assertion of individuality, a stance from which he could, if it is not irreverent to say so, cock a snook at his father and deny all the tiresome business of being Martin's surrogate. This is conjecture and doubtless many other elements entered into his conversion which was a very complete one and which gave him many years of blissful happiness. Hugh's salient characteristic was the way that he flung himself into whatever interested him at the moment. E. F. Benson says that if he were looking for a phrase to describe his brother it would be: "Isn't it fun?" Now his excitement and enthusiasm were directed to the Catholic Church, to his propaganda novels and to the small estate which he purchased at Hare Street near Buntingford. In time the sword outwore the sheath and the Benson neurasthenia claimed its toll, but that was many years ahead.

Mrs Benson, though her own personal religion was perhaps more evangelical than her husband's had been, was far more tolerant of other people's opinions. She felt that every soul must come to God in its own way. So although she asked Hugh to consult various Anglican dignitaries which he duly did to no avail, and never concealed her own beliefs from him, she raised no objections to his course. In fact she felt that their exchange of views, their correspondence, and the confidence which he placed in her brought them nearer together. Nevertheless she stood by her own opinions. "Lucy and I compared the 2 [ordination] services," she wrote, when Hugh poped, "O I AM an Anglican."

○ VIII ○

From about 1903 onwards Tremans entered upon a short halcyon period. Maggie seemed restored in health, busy with her book and her friends, planting the orchard with daffodils, trying to breed peacocks and educating her collie, Taffy. Hugh had obtained a special dispensation from the Pope, allowing him to say Mass in the little chapel on top of the house. ("You must get your mother's permission as well as mine," Pius X reminded him gently.) He immediately brightened up the hitherto Protestant stronghold with Arundel prints and brightly coloured saints painted onto the windows, and adjured Beth, the old nurse now over eighty who supervised the linen, to keep the vestments of the true Church strictly secluded from those of the heretics. Fred was very busy with his own social life—"Fred playing with his Earls and Countesses" as his mother put it, but he, too, was a reasonably frequent visitor, while Arthur made it his second home.

His unpaid fellowship at Magdalene, Cambridge, provided him with rooms in the college and leisure to produce his voluminous literary works and scarcely less voluminous correspondence; but in the long vacations he settled at Tremans, frequently bringing guests; contemporaries such as Edmund Gosse or H. Luxmoore or younger men like George Mallory and Geoffrey Madan.

It was in 1906 that the storm clouds began to gather once more. Mrs Benson, vaguely anxious about

Maggie, went into her room at breakfast time and found her in the grip of a deep depression. She asked what was the matter and Maggie cried: "Oh I am killing it!" The terrible struggle had begun.

On the surface Maggie seemed to recover but by Christmas it was obvious that things were not well. She had one long talk with her mother and spoke of a dread and a darkness, but she told nobody else of her uneasiness. She spent most of the spring of 1906 in the West Country travelling about with Nettie Gourlay and she insisted that she felt much better and "no longer . . . like a piece of old and frayed elastic". She spent the late spring and summer at Tremans. "Oh it's perfect here," she wrote to Hugh, "all the starry sort of flowers are out like white clematis and forget-me-not; do you know the sort of *powdery* look of spring, when all the leaves too are in little knots on the boughs—and the grey parrot . . . and the peacock and the kitten are at the kitchen door—with the bantams close by—the cock bantam had a duel the other day and had to be separated." But behind this fair picture of the visible world she was beginning to feel herself threatened. She yearned for her mother's protection and once more was visited by the conviction that Lucy Tait had stepped in between them and taken her place. She still struggled. Once more she went down to Cornwall and from there she wrote: "I believe the mists will disperse. I think they must. They somehow seem to have risen to hide what is so much better behind them." She stayed in London for a few days on her way home and from there she wrote to her mother a perfectly sane letter saying that she had seen the doctor who was "most re-assuring", that she did not know what to do about Turkeys' Eggs, if there were none locally she must advertise in the *Exchange and Mart* and that she was just off to the Zoo. She also called on her brother Fred in his rooms in Chelsea because she said: "I wanted to see you again first". When she left he began to wonder what "first" could mean. Then she returned to Tremans and wrote to her friend Gladys Bevan that it "was prettier than you can well imagine with cherry trees and tulips and forget-me-nots. . . . I do trust I am serene in spirit when I can realise it—but I couldn't sleep and have a heavy weight of stupidity." Her mother and Lucy had been away but when they returned things got much worse. "The world assumed to her an evil and phantasmal aspect, with the spirits of dreadful beasts and demons lurking behind masked faces of men and women." Mrs Benson telegraphed for her friend and family doctor, Ross Todd, who arrived that evening, "He persuaded her [Maggie] to act normally, and dress for dinner and come down, and he promised to defend her and others from herself. Before dinner was over the crash came; violent homicidal mania took possession of her."*

She was removed to a home for the insane and for the next ten years she was never out of the doctor's hands. She became better. She was placed under the care of a doctor at Wimbledon and had a certain amount of liberty but she could never come home for she cherished an undying antipathy to her mother and Lucy Tait. Just once after a severe illness, when pre-

* None of the accounts show precisely what form this took. Did she assault her mother or Lucy Tait? And with what weapon? The carving knife?

sumably her guardians thought her incapable of much physical activity, she gave them the slip, travelled down by train to Horsted Keynes and walked up to Tremans where a young guest of Arthur's, Geoffrey Madan, looked up suddenly to see a strange white face pressed against the glass of the drawing-room window. The Bensons, he said, took the situation with admirable calm. They went to greet her. Mrs Benson showed her her own bedroom, kept just as she had left it. She spent the night there and next morning the doctor from Wimbledon came to take her away. She acquiesced.

It was during these sad years that Fred Benson showed at his best. Mrs Benson could no longer penetrate the clouds that hung around Maggie. "It is very difficult, Dearest, for me to know what you like hearing," she wrote pathetically. "I try different subjects but just now nothing seems to please you. Oh my darling I know this isn't the *real you* but some little darkness that you allow to come between us. . . . Your real self is there, I know, but doesn't show itself just now." E. F. Benson wrote that when he went through his mother's papers after her death he found many of Maggie's bitter letters to her and that he was surprised she had kept them for "she knew that they were no more than symptoms of Maggie's disorder, and not herself". He must have destroyed them for they are no longer among the Benson papers. One letter survives from Mrs Benson to Maggie describing the death of the old nurse and it is annotated by Maggie with comments in tiny little squeezed up writing such as: "I did not agree" or simply "No".

Neither could Arthur Benson be of much help, for

he himself became affected by Maggie's melancholia and for two years he remained in a neurasthenic state, suffering from what he termed "a nausea of the spirit", unable to enjoy anything in life. After he had recovered, he used sometimes to take Maggie out to tea, to see a picture gallery or a museum but on one occasion she refused to go back. She was quite quiet about it and her nurse soon over-persuaded her but it scared him and he would not risk it again.

Fred, however, became Maggie's prop and stand-by. After his move to London he had been rather the odd-man-out in the Benson family. Arthur and Hugh had formed a close relationship and Fred seemed to them "both dilettante and frivolous." "They regarded London and the social gatherings which I so much frequented with an amazed horror," he wrote, "and when obliged to go there fled back at the earliest possible moment to Cambridge or Hare Street."

Maggie seems to have shared their attitude. "In one way this odd outburst of books, in an unmarrying family, is better than marriage," she wrote to her brother Arthur. "After all, marriage does loosen the original family tie, whereas here—at any rate with you and Hugh, who express yourselves and not the reflection of your environment in your books—one gets to know you in a double way, by a sort of second channel." This seems to have been a back-handed slap at Fred but now in the time of her tribulation the old relationship was restored. They had been the closest of allies in the old nursery days. They had kept an aquarium together, they had cherished and lost a stickleback, they had planned and even begun a novel in which Fred in later days saw the first faint outlines of *Dodo*.* Now it was in this world that Maggie cared to live. "Her memory was absolutely unimpaired," Fred wrote, "and by the hour we talked over detail after detail of the days when as children we made joint collections of plants and butterflies and birds' eggs. Always after a visit I received next day a letter recalling other memories which our talk had slipped, the finding of the night-jar's nest, the capture of the first 'Clouded Yellow'." But her mind remained darkened; Fred describes it as "liquid and clear" but with the surface covered by a "grey ice of delusion", and the chief of her delusions was that by plots and contrivances her mother was keeping her away from home. There was one small break in the clouds; she suffered a heart attack and as she recovered, for a few hours her mind was serene and normal and she asked to see her mother but the clouds returned thicker than ever. Then in May, 1916, she once more became seriously ill. Fred visited her and found her delusions were "thick and dense". She felt that there were several people, "not quite people", lurking in corners, talking and conspiring against her. He went away and when he returned the next day the clouds had parted. Maggie was her old self. She sent for her mother, who came,

* The novel was centred round a character who was all-wise all-good, all-comprehending and who was based on their adored mother. Faint vestigial traces of this character may be found in the Mrs Vivian of *Dodo*, and if anyone ever reads this out-of-date novel they may well be puzzled by the placing of Mrs Vivian who seems to have been intended by the author as a central character but who never becomes one. This gives the explanation. In *Dodo the Second* Mrs Vivian has become rather deaf "which somehow reduced her importance". Mrs Benson also became rather deaf at the end of her life. This little sentence seems to show a rather curious sort of insensitivity.

and they never spoke of the past nine years, or of Lucy Tait, but went back to that old time when they had been close together in unclouded love. When Mrs Benson left her she promised to come again very early the next morning and Maggie went to bed in good time in order she said to be ready for the visit. She woke in the night and the nurse heard her repeat the first verse of the hymn:

As pants the hart for cooling streams.

Then she went to sleep again and died in her sleep.

○ IX ○

After Maggie's death Arthur, yielding to the Benson temptation to embalm the past in words, started to write a book called: *The Life and Letters of Maggie Benson*. This was an ill-advised venture. He had attributed his first attack of neurasthenia to the shock it gave him to see Maggie after her collapse and Fred hazards the guess that, feeling himself threatened for so many years, he intended the book to act as a sort of therapy, which would enable him to look the fear in the face and show it had no longer any force. It had precisely the opposite effect. Dwelling so much on Maggie and her mental instability pulled him down into the depths and once more he slid into melancholy, a far more serious attack, which lasted for a much longer period. "For six whole years," he wrote in 1923, "I have awakened *every* morning with a sickening pang, just wondering if I could get through the barest outline of a day, with incredible effort—and all the time struggling with a sort of outrageous nausea for life and all its concerns and occupations."

All the Bensons suffered from neurasthenia. As we have seen, even the cheerful and reliable Nellie had her 'black moods'. David Newsome attributes Martin's somewhat uneven progress at school (he alternated bursts of the greatest brilliance with periods of lying fallow) to the same manic depressive moods characteristic of the rest of the family. Hugh Benson died more or less from overwork, exhausted by his writing

205

and his lecture tours, but the ceaseless effort had some compulsive element in it. He himself compared it to his father's need to bury himself in continual never-ceasing activity. Yet there was more than that to it. Father Martindale, in the official life of Monsignor Benson, more or less admits as much. "His brain was as restless as ever." Martindale wrote, describing a retreat Hugh made to the Abbey of Caldey a month before his death. "He could not for a moment cease from constructing plots and working out new novels; even at Mass their ingenious developments would harass him. His anxiety raced onwards, at times into panic. He believed himself the victim of obsession. But I have no duty to relate these moments of extreme humiliation: it is enough to say that the spectre of acute neurasthenia began to haunt him, and to recall, more threatening than ever, the conviction that his collapse would be soon, sudden, and complete."

It was perhaps fortunate for Hugh that the collapse, when it came, proved to be a physical one. He died of pneumonia supervening on false angina, with a perfectly clear mind. Arthur in his biographical study gives a moving account of the death-bed and of Hugh's last words: "I commit my soul to God, to Mary and to Joseph," but he breaks out in his private note-book with the comment: "R. H. B. in his last moments praying to *Joseph*".

Fred Benson was the one of the family who suffered least from these black moods. Yet it is he who leaves the most vivid account of what the depression was truly like. He describes how he went to bed one evening in normal spirits and when he woke "the Thing was there . . . in my bed and about my path, and in my breakfast, there was a blackening poison that spread and sprouted like some infernal mushroom of plague". He went down to Kew with a beloved friend and "his face and his presence were no more than the face and presence of any stranger in the street. He had lost his meaning, he was nonsense. . . . We looked at the flaring towers of golden and russet leaf and I saw them as you see something through the wrong end of a telescope. I saw them through glass, through a diving bell. Everything was no more than dried flowers sapless, brittle and colourless." He also describes the intense sense of loneliness which encompassed him. "I was alone, as I had always been alone; here was the truth of it, for it was but a fancy figment that there was a scheme, a connection, a knitting of the members of the world to each other and of them to God. I had made that up myself. . . . But I knew better now; I was alone and all was said."

This black despondency was surely hereditary, a legacy from the Archbishop, but it was not the only thing that marked out the Bensons as abnormal. It is surely strange that the five grown-up members of the family, with the doubtful exception for a short while of Maggie, never for one moment showed any interest in any person of the opposite sex. This sexual deviancy may have been inherited from the Sidgwick side; it may have been encouraged by their sheltered bringing-up which made them shrink from any too close complete relationship away from their family nest, and by their overdependence on their mother. It is impossible to say. Nevertheless, the facts remain.

We have seen how both Nellie and Maggie formed fervently romantic friendships at college; how the former had, apparently with her mother's blessing, began a more adult relationship with the composer Ethel Smyth; and how Maggie after a short, wistful glance towards more normal things had become immersed in two feminine friendships with Nettie Gourlay and Gladys Bevan. The brothers were equally incapable of heterosexual relationships. Both Arthur and Hugh actively disliked women; but whereas Arthur occasionally toyed with the idea, not exactly of marriage but of how pleasant it would have been if he had once got married to some absolutely charming creature, Hugh found the whole business of marriage repellent and "quite inconceivable".

All three brothers had homosexual tendencies. Probably with Arthur anyway these remained suppressed. It is doubtful whether he ever got beyond the stage of sentimental friendship with various beautiful and intelligent young men, many of them completely heterosexual. "The one supreme happiness of my life just now," he wrote when he was forty-eight, "is my friendship with several young men on really equal terms"; and friendship with a romantic flavour was probably just what it was. He was also cautious. "I'm a little anxious," he wrote to a younger friend, who had obviously received a declaration of affection from some third party, "I hope you won't *write* anything in reply. . . . It's a difficult region and the slime pits so close to the road—and such fine and happy emotions, which suddenly develop poisons, as rabbit pies develop ptomaine. . . . Don't think I am prim or prudish— I'm neither; but I have seen such nasty messes, and such unhappy and indelible contact with tar brushes. "I am glad you say so simply what has happened to him—and shall I say frankly it is just what has happened to myself, only with a difference? . . . I don't know what puts and keeps things straight; cleanness and humour and an absence of the hectic qualities." It is true that Fred on going through Arthur's papers after his death found what he described as "a packet of letters of very dangerous stuff", and another "that had to be burnt unopened",* but the whole drift of Arthur's diary† and letters seems to indicate that caution prevailed. He was sexually very low-keyed. The following is a typical entry. "I sit wishing that W. [Winterbotham] were back every minute—and yet with a curious self-sufficiency and serenity which, when I am well, tides me over emotional crises. I don't like being thus at all—it is hard and cold; but it has always been so with me, and I have suffered very little through my emotions in this life."

"He began and continued and ended," wrote Percy Lubbock, "under the restraint of something shy, prudent, mistrustful—something which he clearly perceived and greatly disliked but which held him." "There was always a barrier," wrote his brother Fred, "a keep in the centre of his fortress into which he could retreat, barring the door behind him. It was no use knocking at it, for no answer came, or, at the most, an upper window was opened and a few dozen words sent the would-be intruder about his business."

Both Arthur and Hugh seem to have drifted through Eton without much enlargement of their emotional life. Eton appears to have had a great tradition of

---

* Why did Fred record this? It is a further instance of the queer Benson psychology.

† Though it is true that we have only a small portion of this.

laissez-faire. Some boys had homosexual relations, some didn't. Nobody was shocked on the one hand or persecuted on the the other. Fred on the other hand, who went to Marlborough, plunged immediately into an intensely exciting world of fervent schoolboy feelings. These, embarrassingly displayed, may be found by anyone who cares to look in the pages of *David Blaize* or *Our Family Affairs.* The following snatch of dialogue from the latter book will sufficiently indicate the style and tempo.

> "It will be awful rot without you." [Fred was just leaving Marlborough.]
> "You'll soon find somebody else," said I.
> "Funny," said he.
> "Laugh then," said I.
> "It's been ripping anyhow," he said. "Did two fellows ever have such a good time?"
> "Never. Nor will. And there's chapel bell. Get up."
> "Psalms this morning," he said telegraphically.
> "I know. 'Brethren and companions sake.' Didn't think you had noticed!"
> "Rather. Good old Psalm."

The verisimilitude of this nauseous extract is well attested by E. F. Benson's diary for 1885-91. 1886 seems to be chiefly occupied with the fluctuations of his friendship for one Risley. June was a particularly fervid month as the following extracts show:

"June 10th. It is now 12.30 and here I am feeling hopeless about Risley. What on earth am I to do?" The next day the entry is simply "Quarrel Risley". The following day it was made up and Tennyson— "the blessings on the falling out that all the more endears"—is quoted. The 12th of July features simply:

RISLEY, and on the following Sunday there is Holy Communion RISLEY. On July 26th comes the entry that the next pages are closed with sealing-wax and are always to be left unread. (Later they were, more prudently, torn out.) The following year this enthusiasm for Risley seems to yield to a penchant for Glennie: "I have felt towards him as I have never felt towards anyone else," and in 1888 the beloved is Vincent. "I feel perfectly mad about him just now but I hope and believe it will soon be all right. Ah if he only knew, and yet I think he does; it is happier than all others, for I have no reason to regret anything."

E. F. Benson was at Cambridge by this time and it is obvious from his novels (*David of King's, Robin Linnet, The Babe B. A.* etc.) that these romantic friendships lasted all through his University days. They may, perhaps, have been little more than a hangover from the sentimental public-school atmosphere of eroticism laced with religion. In later life, however, it seems probable, though we have no actual proof, that he indulged in more emancipated relationships. He was more highly sexed than either of his brothers and he was also more of a man of the world. He had escaped from cloister and college, acquired such friends as Phil Burne-Jones,* Francis Yeats Brown† and John Ellingham Brooks‡ (with whom he shared a villa on Capri) and probably enjoyed an adult sexual life.

* Sir Philip Burne-Jones, 1861-1926, 2nd Bart. Son of the well-known artist, Edward Burne-Jones.
† Francis Yeats Brown, 1886-1944, author of *Bengal Lancer.*
‡ John Ellingham Brooks, a rich dilettante who lived in Capri. Harold Acton describes him as "a queer Englishman who encouraged [his wife] to dress as a boy".

Moreover, one feels that had he lived in the present more permissive age he would have been glad to get rid of all the tiresome business of concealment. His books are riddled with hints both about himself and his family. The blurb of *Up and Down*, which he must have passed even if he did not write it, states that: "Fact and fiction are skilfully interwoven around the central lives of two men and their friendship." In *Mother* and in *Final Edition* he almost tells us outright about his mother's relationship with Lucy Tait. Unlike Maggie he never seems to have been jealous yet it was perhaps his devotion to his mother that geared his emotional development. He describes in *Our Family Affairs* how he used to stroke her hair while she read Dickens aloud to the children an hour before bedtime. He must have been about seven and "her voice and the contact of my fingers on her hair wakened in me the knowledge of how I loved her". He resented his father's treatment of her. "E. C. [Edward Cantuar] is sometimes brutal to M. B." he wrote in his diary when he was still a schoolboy at Marlborough, and after their father's death he did for a while do his best to fill the vacant place. "Fred was as tender as a child," Mrs Benson wrote in her diary, "as loving and strong as a husband and as sensitive as a woman. He only wanted not to disappoint me and he told me one evg. he could never marry he loved me too much."

Hugh was as averse to women, except for his mother and his old nurse, as either of his brothers. "Of marriage he loathed the thought," wrote Father Martindale, "from congenital instinct, unless I err, and perhaps more significantly so than if this abhorrence he had been merely the result of ascetical speculation." He was never, in fact, very close to any human being of either sex. "His [Hugh's] religion appears to be totally disassociated with anything to do with humanity," Maggie wrote and in Fred's opinion "the human race ... were playmates and companions, interesting but not individually absorbing. In the whole course of his life he only formed one intimacy which had this quality, and disastrous was the end of it."

So much has been written on the subject of this "disastrous intimacy" that it will only be treated very briefly in these pages. In 1905 Monsignor Benson (as he then was) wrote to a comparatively unknown writer who sometimes signed himself 'Fr. Rolfe' and sometimes 'Baron Corvo', congratulating him on his book, *Hadrian VII*. This led to a friendship and correspondence which involved, according to Father Martindale, "letters not only weekly, but at times daily, and of an intimate character, exhaustingly charged with emotion". Unfortunately Father Martindale destroyed these letters! The friendship survived a joint walking tour and a visit to Mrs Benson's house where Arthur was present and cast a somewhat blighting influence. It finally broke up, as did all Rolfe's friendships, in bitterness and recrimination. The fault was undoubtedly Hugh's. They had agreed to write a joint novel about St Thomas à Becket. Hugh, possibly under orders from his Church, which understandably found Rolfe a character likely to "cause scandal", then made the suggestion that though they should share profits Rolfe's name should not appear on the title page. Rolfe was furious at this, and with some reason— Benson, though an inferior writer, was a best-seller and the known collaboration would have helped on Rolfe's limping literary career. Finally the whole project was abandoned and Rolfe was left firing off those abusive post-cards and letters with which anyone in his circle was so familiar. Benson stuck them up on his mantelpiece and said loftily: "Of course I am sorry that he should be such a beast, but I can't help that." Materially Rolfe suffered more and complained louder but it may have been Benson who underwent the most emotional damage. Rolfe had had other friends, other *crises d'amour*, other shattered hopes. For Benson this was the one emotional entanglment, perhaps the only time that his heart was really touched.* It is interesting to compare their two fictional assessments of the friendships. Rolfe depicts Benson in *The Desire and Pursuit of the Whole* as Monsignor Bobugo Bonson, a little stuttering priest, wearing paper collars and a black straw Alpine hat, with a habit of saying 'I know' between every sentence, and an overweening affection for money. It is a mildly funny caricature, resembling the original, but it is done entirely from the outside. The most casual acquaintance might have depicted Robert Hugh Benson so. Benson draws Rolfe's portrait twice, once as Chris Dell in *The Sentimentalists*, once as Enid Bessington in *Initiation*. The former is a story with a slightly unpleasant flavour, in which Chris

---

* The only other person who seems to have got past Hugh's defences was a little boy called Ken Lindsay, with whose care Hugh was for some reason charged. "Hugh's love of children was very great," wrote Arthur Benson, ". . . and [he] filled a part of Hugh's life as nothing else did." However, according to Arthur, "Circumstances arose which made it necessary that Ken should go". No further details are given and Father Martindale's *Life* does not mention Ken Lindsay.

is finally redeemed by being '*broken*'* by a rich old Catholic recluse who gives him a job as an under-gardener, forcing him to undertake hard manual labour, to touch his cap and behave like a servant. Chris, who is enticed into this by a skilful playing on his *amour propre* ("You say you only want an opportunity to earn an honest living but you wouldn't have the guts to stick it"), seems to be partially hypnotised into remaining in this ridiculous situation and finally emerges, clear-eyed, clean-washed and saved. Benson did, in fact, invite Rolfe to live at Hare Street to look after the garden and the poultry in exchange for his keep and a small wage. It may have been a genuine attempt to solve the problem of an intractable and penniless Rolfe who insisted on staying in Venice, but Rolfe certainly saw it in a different light. The offer was made through Pirie-Gordon and Rolfe wrote to him as follows: "You just sit down . . . and read Bobugo's book *The Sensiblist* over again. You'll find my reason there . . . for refusing the offer of which his sadimaniac effrontery makes your blank ineptitude the medium. . . . No thank you: I will not incarcerate myself in the lonely country-house dungeon of a despot, whose fixed idea is to break in pieces men's minds and natures by physical torment and mental torture, so that he may gum them together again on a model of his own and exhibit them . . . as perfect cures, all for his own greater glory."

But the picture of Rolfe as Chris Dell in *The Sentimentalists* pales in interest before the portrait of Rolfe in *Initiation*. Here Rolfe is translated into Enid Bessington, a beautiful girl with whom the hero of the

* Benson was a great believer in the 'breaking' process.

book is deeply in love.* The book was published in 1914 only a year before Hugh's death and it shows that he had Rolfe much on his mind. Benson more or less admitted the identification and it is fascinating to leaf through the early part of *Initiation* with this in mind. One imagines that the wildly dangerous pact Nevill and Enid made to tell each other their faults was founded on fact and it is certain that the final blinding quarrel between them conveys Benson's view of Rolfe and of their relationship. On this occasion Enid, in a typically Rolfeian fashion, throws up to Nevill all the tiny causes of offence of which he had been quite unaware but which had rankled and festered in her mind.

"But what held him," Benson concluded, ". . . in something very like horror, was the shocking change in her whole character from that which he had previously believed it to be: it was as if a mask had been torn suddenly away and a frightful face disclosed. He had thought her very nearly sublime—unlike others, spiritual, aloof, unique. He had thought her markedly self-controlled, of an exquisiteness transcendent of that which breeding could give, tolerant, charitable, even great. He had loved this presentment that he had seen—loved it as he had never loved any human being before, to his knowledge: he had thought she understood him perfectly; he had hoped humbly and simply that he was learning to understand her.

"Yet now, in an instant, a terrifying kind of coarseness disclosed itself; she snarled at him; she framed, as

* I am enormously indebted to Mr Brian Fothergill's essay 'A Friendship's Downfall' published in *New Quests for Corvo*, Icon Books Ltd, 1965.

well as she could, sentences and phrases with the
object of giving as much pain as possible; she tortured
things and words into sinister intentions that never
crossed his mind. He was as one who goes to kiss his
wife and is met by a devil's changeling."

This is no portrait from the outside like Chris Dell
with his intaglio ring and his habit of saying "dear
Man", or like Bobugo Bonson with his stutter and his
Mad Hatter's face. It is the testimony of someone
who has been deeply hurt. Could Corvo have read
Initiation, little as he would have liked the identification of himself with a woman, he would have been
glad of that much.

One other interest which was shared by nearly all
the Benson family was the guidance of other people's
souls. This they derived not, as might be expected, from
their clerical father but from their mother, Arthur
Benson in one of his essays writes of the "natural
priesthood of women", and there is little doubt that
he was thinking of his mother.* Gifted with keen
psychological insight and knowing that she herself
had enormously benefited by the ministrations of 'Tau',
Mrs Benson felt it not only her pleasure but her duty
to give others the care that, in these days, they receive
from a psychiatrist. "Her master passion," wrote
Ethel Smyth, "was undoubtedly the care of souls. A

* Mrs Benson used actually to give seminars on Holy Writ.
Constance Sitwell, in her autobiography, *Bright Morning*, includes
a passage which seems to sum up the whole atmosphere of
Anglican Episcopal life. "I spent the day with Bishops and
Archbishops," she wrote, "sorting books for Cousin Edward
[Talbot, Bishop of Southwark] in the morning and going to
Lambeth with Winnie to hear Mrs Benson speak on the Epistle
to the Hebrews."

great part of her life was consecrated to her patients, as I used to call them, who when bereft of her physical presence were kept going by words of counsel and comfort written on letter paper so diminutive that it inevitably suggested a prescription."

This passion for soul guidance descended to her children. Martin had impressed his father by helping to prepare his sisters for their confirmation. These sisters in their turn helped and encouraged their college friends. Maggie "never shrank from advising and even urging strongly those who seemed in danger of taking a wrong turn and who appealed to her for guidance," wrote one of these.

The shining exception to this psychological meddling was Fred. He was much less what the schoolboy jargon of his day would have designated as 'pi' than any of the rest of his family. Indeed a study of his books reveals a deep antipathy to church services, to clerical jokes and to the whole apparatus of conventional religion. As far as spiritual growth was concerned he was perfectly contented to live and let live, but the same cannot be said for either of his brothers.

Hugh of course, with his vocation as a priest, may have felt it his duty to offer spiritual help and guidance. Yet the enormous bulk of his correspondence and his involvement with so many lady penitents, was probably dictated by his own nature rather than the advice of his own Church. His Church, moreover, would surely have questioned some of his methods. He "had quite a definite opinion of the value of 'consecrated bullying'," wrote Father Martindale. "He once announced to a friend the appalling dogma that it was impossible to do anything with a woman until you

had made her cry. This same friend was once privileged to behold the operation in process, and to
watch a sullen servant maid systematically reduced to
tears, until, realising who was her master, she was
converted to docility." Arthur Benson strongly ob-
jected to the feminine 'fans', there is really no other
word, who clustered round Hugh. He felt that by
their demands they had contributed to the overwork
which brought on his end, and when he came to
administer Hugh's literary estate and to undertake
his biography he wrote very sharply about them. "Just
at present I am like Pentheus, the prey of Dionysiac
elderly Roman Catholic females," is a passage in one
of his letters and again: "In dealing with Hugh's
affairs I seem to have disturbed a brood of *earwigs*".

"I was engaged all yesterday," he wrote, "in trying
to tear off the serpents, like Laocoön—d--n these
women! There were half a dozen who sucked my
brother's blood and now they suck mine."

His own fans, who so much admired the tranquil,
gentle prose of his essays and the benign, scholarly
figure of their author, would have been considerably
astonished by these comments; for he himself, with
less excuse than Hugh who was after all a professional,
had set up as a sort of Father Confessor to innumerable
middle-aged ladies consoling them with letters full of
beautiful uplift. "I have become the beloved author of
a feminine tea-party kind of audience," he wrote to
Geoffrey Madan; "the mild and low-spirited people
who would like to think the world a finer place than
they have any reason for doing." A very typical letter
is one which he wrote to an unknown undergraduate
at Aberdeen University in 1911. "Many thanks for

your kind letter," he began. "I am very glad that my books have pleased you and still more that they have been of some use.

"I don't think life is given us in order that we may discover things, but to live it—and our best discoveries are not the things we mean to discover. It grows, I find, more interesting as I get older; and experience, however disagreeable, has generally some fine message to deliver. I don't think it is a good thing to get ourselves to interrogate the insoluble, though one can't escape the eye of the Sphinx, which follows us over the desert ridges."

It was probably with some such anodyne words of wisdom that he replied to the first letter of Mrs de Nottbeck, an ardent American fan, married to a rich European and living in Switzerland. Very quickly however, their correspondence became warmer and more intimate. He confided about his neurasthenic illnesses; he told her of his plans and hopes for Magdalene. Suddenly she offered him a small fortune, £40,000, with more to come, to be entirely at his own disposal. Naturally he demurred but she urged it, saying that all her family concurred, and eventually he accepted. Their correspondence continued but they never met. The end of this odd relationship was that after Arthur's death she and his brother Fred joined together to erect a window to Arthur's memory in Rye Church where it stands today, embodying the names and arms of the two donors.

Arthur Benson died in 1925; Mrs Benson had predeceased her two surviving sons in 1918; and now Fred was left alone, a short, rather soldierly-looking figure with a clipped grey moustache and the curiously bright, large blue eyes which he had inherited from his father. In spite of crippling arthritis he enjoyed life in the house at Rye which had once belonged to Henry James, acting as Mayor of the town and writing his amusing books about Miss Mapp and Queen Lucia.* This series, which are probably the only books by any of the Archbishop's family read at the present day, is a mannered comedy revolving round two middle-aged ladies and set mostly at Rye. They make no pretensions to humanity, the figures are cardboard cut-outs, but they are very gaily and skilfully painted and both Lucia with her cultural pretensions and Miss Mapp with her devastating curiosity about her neighbour's affairs, are often extremely funny.

These novels command a small but steadily growing band of devotees but to my mind more valuable is the last volume of autobiography, *Final Edition*, whose proofs E. F. Benson corrected before he went into a nursing-home in 1940, to die under the surgeon's knife.

There we find his assessment of himself and of his unusual, puzzling and fascinating family. Anyone interested in the Bensons should read it. He was, of course, too close and too involved to set down the whole truth, even as he knew it; therefore there is room for a later biographer to add, to assess and to deduce. Yet when all is said and done the Bensons remain an enigma. They had so many gifts but there is something twisted about them, something lacking, as if the pressures of their diversely endowed parents had been too much for them; as if they had never emerged from

* *Queen Lucia, Miss Mapp, Lucia in London, Lucia's Progress, Mapp and Lucia, Trouble for Lucia.*

their adolescence, remaining, on some deeper level, maimed and unfulfilled. The Archbishop once thanked Heaven for his "noble children". They would surely have disclaimed such an epithet. Arthur's own summing-up of himself and his family seems more appropriate. "I suppose we all have a touch of something morbid and not quite controlled—" he wrote in his diary—"as Maggie's collapse shows—which Papa had, but coupled in him with great physical strength. There is a touch of diseased self-consciousness about us all, I think."

NOTES

The unpublished papers which I have used for the first section of this book are all included in the Strachey Trust Papers, as yet uncatalogued, to which I refer as STP. Besides family papers these papers include an essay by Lytton Strachey entitled *Lancaster Gate*, the typescript of an autobiography by Lady Strachey entitled *Some Recollections*, and the typescript of a collection of tributes to and reminiscences of Lady Strachey, obviously compiled at the time of her death and headed *J.M.S.* These three sources I have referred to as LG/STP, Some Recollections/STP., and JMS/STP. Some of the recollections were published by Lady Strachey in the *Nation and Athenaeum*, parts of the *J.M.S.* material have been quoted by Michael Holroyd in *Lytton Strachey*, and the whole of *Lancaster Gate* has been published in *Lytton Strachey By Himself*, edited by Michael Holroyd. In all cases I have taken my quotations direct from the Strachey Papers.

The main source of unpublished material in the second section comes from the Benson Deposit in the Bodleian Library. Items from this source I have marked B/D followed by the appropriate numbers. I have also had access to Archbishop Benson's diaries which are in the Wren Library, Trinity College, Cambridge, to E. F. Benson's diary, written when he was at Marlborough and Cambridge, which is in the possession of Mr Kenneth Rose, and to A. C. Benson's letters to Geoffrey Madan. The originals of these are in the Pepys Library, Magdalene College, Cambridge, but I was able to see the typescript copies by kind permission of Mrs Geoffrey Madan.

Published books about the Bensons are plentiful, nearly all written by themselves. I have in most cases given the full title but in the interests of brevity I have referred to the *Life of Edward White Benson Archbishop of Canterbury* by A. C. Benson as *Life*, to the *Life of Monsignor Robert Hugh Benson* by Father Martindale S.J. as Martindale, and to the *Life and Letters of Maggie Benson* by A. C. Benson as *Maggie*.

REFERENCES

In most cases only the first few words of each reference are quoted here

FOREWORD

Page Line

12   13   "Bertrand Russell was there"—A. C. Benson's *Diary* edited by Percy Lubbock, 18.1.1919.

12   26   "the earlier estate of their ancestors"—Martindale, Vol. I, p. 84.

13   17   "Your father at breakfast"—Mrs Benson to Maggie Benson. Undated B/D 3/60.

THE STRACHEYS

I

Page Line

17   1   "Lancaster Gate . . . is a . . ."—*The Buildings of England—London*, pp. 307, 308.

18   17   "a dome of pink and white glass"—LG/STP.

18   29   "When we lived in Lancaster Gate"—JMS/STP.

20   ftn.   Virginia Woolf remembers—JMS/STP.

20   1   When "six or seven Stracheys"—*Sowing* by Leonard Woolf, pp. 207-8.

21   8   "Your Papa and I are actually alone"—Lady Strachey to Pernel, STP.

21   18   "My ideal"—JMS/STP.

21   24   "The Kingdon fiend"—Pippa to Pernel, STP.

22   5   "The Squire"—Dorothy to Pippa, 1892, STP.

22   11   ". . . the painful scene"—Lady Strachey to Pippa, 19.10.00, STP.

22   20   . . . returned anticipating "a delicious supper"—Lady Strachey to Pippa, 20.12.01, STP.

22   27   the various butlers—LG/STP.

23   24   "filth packets"—Ibid.

REFERENCES

Page	Line	
31	11	". . . just the colours of a wasp"—Some Recollections/ STP.
31	22	"Your father is getting along"—Lady Strachey to Ralph, 1901, STP.
32	31	"The reelers continue to reel"—Pippa to Lytton. Only dated Monday but probably 1902, STP.
33	8	"he was extraordinarily friendly and charming"— Sowing by Leonard Woolf, p. 205.
33	16	"visualize distinctly Aunt Janie's expression—JMS./ STP.
34	25	"You know I suppose that he is to go to India"—Sir Richard to James, 12.3.98, STP.
35	16	". . . horribly persecuted by the most vicious indigestion"—Sir Richard to Pippa, 12.5.01, STP.
36	13	"It was my mother who counted"—Dorothy Strachey to Norah Smallwood.
36	32	". . . it was my pride and delight"—Some Recollections/STP.
37	14	"This is an impossible pace"—Ibid.
37	18	". . . took a turn . . . for old times' sake."—Ibid.
37	29	"Her chief passion in life was public affairs".—Olivia by Dorothy Strachey, p. 12.
38	4	"the first glimpse of the naked machinery".—"Consequences" in Plain Tales From the Hills by Rudyard Kipling.
38	29	Very often of black satin—JMS./STP.
38	31	"She would walk into the room"—Sowing by Leonard Woolf, p. 205.
39	32	"the guarded road like a wide ribbon"—Lady Strachey to Pippa, 8.2.01, STP.
41	11	"An International Song"—STP.
42	7	"passionately intellectual"—Sowing by Leonard Woolf, p. 205.

III

REFERENCES

Page Line

49 22 "It would be difficult"—Oliver to Pernel, 25.10.00, STP.

49 29 "How like Margaret"—Lady Strachey to Pippa, 5.5.14, STP.

50 11 "I had a talk with him this morning"—Lady Strachey to Pippa, 10.2.98, STP.

50 23 "The great pain of this place"—Oliver to Pernel, 1899, STP.

50 31 "As you don't know India"—Oliver to Pernel, 8.3.00, STP.

51 20 "My dearest Folderol"—Pippa to Lytton undated, but 2.2.97 subsequently added, STP.

51 24 "I have a great many entertaining ancedotes"—Pippa to Lytton, 2.8.95, STP.

51 32 "Lytton Lytton To you I must direct my Wail"—Ibid., 8.1.00.

52 23 "how soon the news could spread abroad"—Lytton to Maynard Keynes. Quoted *Lytton Strachey* (Holroyd), Vol. I. Chap. 5.

53 6 "I got a strange letter from Lytton"—Oliver to Pernel, 8.2.00, STP.

53 14 "Do you think—we are so happy together"—Related by Philippa Strachey to Lucy Norton.

54 7 "I find that Duncan has sent off his letter"—Lytton to Pippa, dated "Tuesday" 1906, STP.

54 25 "When he was read Macaulay's lines—Some Recollections/STP.

55 ftn. Pippa told Carrington—*Lytton Strachey* (Holroyd), Vol. II.

55 19 "I have just this moment heard of Faure's death"— James to Lady Strachey, 12.2.99, STP.

56 1 "I have always thought Jembeau"—Lady Strachey to Pernel, 29.10.96, STP.

REFERENCES

Page	Line	
63	24	"Dearest Lyt"—Dorothy to Lytton, 8.2.03, STP. Quoted Holroyd, Vol. I, p. 177.
64	8	"Hurra! hurra! great joy and delight"—Lady Strachey to Pernel, 6.12.99, STP.
64	15	"Bussy the painter"—Dorothy to Lytton, 2.12.00, STP.
64	17	"The chief amusement at present"—Dorothy to Pippa, 21.11.01, STP.
65	9	"You will doubtless be more astonished than pleased"—Lady Strachey to Lytton, 8.2.03, STP. Quoted Holroyd, Vol. I, p. 177.
65	21	"It seems so dreadfully tantalising"—Dorothy to Lady Strachey, 4.4.05, STP.
65	30	"I am sometimes very homesick for all of you"—Ibid., 24.3.05, STP.
66	7	"Don't give us up"—Vanessa Bell to Pippa, 10.4.41, STP.
66	17	Ruby's "shield and buckler"—Oliver to Pippa, 1.5.00, STP.
66	21	"My dear angel and stand-by"—Lady Strachey to Pippa, 18.5.19, STP.
66	25	"More profoundly and universally a person of good-will"—*The Journey Not the Arrival Matters* (Woolf), p. 120.
67	14	"All that valley"—Roger Fry to Pippa, 15.6.15, STP.
67	29	Philippa Strachey told a friend—Conversation with Lucy Norton.
68	7	"My Melvillian picture has arrived"—Pippa to Pernel, 6.11.95, STP.
68	25	"You can imagine my despair"—Ibid., 21.5.95, STP.
69	12	"as she could not penetrate the riddle of existence"—Dorothy to Pippa, 21.11.93, STP.
69	24	"They play a mean and wildly exasperating game"—Rupert Brooke to Geoffrey Keynes. Quoted in *Rupert Brooke* by Christopher Hassall, p. 69.

TWO VICTORIAN FAMILIES

REFERENCES

V

Page	Line	
79	13	"We all send our love to"—Lady Strachey to Pippa, 1900, STP.
79	23	"to marry an unknown person"—Pippa to Lady Strachey, 22.10.00, STP.
80	16	with "awe and respect"—Ibid., 14.11.01, STP.
80	24	"My dearest, darling Papa,"—Pippa to Sir Richard. Undated but postmarked Simla, 19.9.01, STP.
81	5	"We have been horror-struck"—Lady Strachey to Pippa, 1.2.01, STP.
81	15	"What society in general"—Pippa to Lady Strachey. Undated, probably Jan. 1901, STP.
81	25	her liver—"may its name be degraded"—Ibid., 31.1.01, STP.
82	1	"Nobody who has not seen it"—Lady Strachey to Pippa, 8.2.01, STP.
82	6	"With one accord"—Pippa to Lady Strachey, 25.1.01, STP.
82	8	"The wretched shops"—Ibid., 25.1.01, STP.
82	15	"A black chiffon hat"—Dorothy to Pippa, 28.2.01, STP.
83	18	"a wild and confused mass"—Ibid., 23.4.01, STP.
84	6	"exhausted with fatigue"—Ibid., 4.5.01, STP.
84	1	When the hour of the funeral was fixed—Ibid., STP.
84	25	"She wasted no time in argument"—The whole account of the funeral and the cremation which follows was given by Philippa Strachey to Lucy Norton.
86	27	"The servants and people are all very sweet"—Pippa to Lady Strachey, 8.8.01, STP.
87	13	"translated by Tulsi"—Ibid., STP.
87	32	"PRIVATE & CONFIDENTIAL"—Ibid., undated, probably July 1901, STP.

REFERENCES

Page Line

99   11   Aunt Hennie shared the charming house—Information
          given to the author by Duncan Grant.

99   23   "truly kind and most anxious"—Lady Strachey to
          Pippa, 6.12.01, STP.

100   3   "Aunt Henrietta was suddenly seized"—Lady Strachey
          8.8.05, STP.

100   9   "She . . . remarked that it was very wicked"—Pernel
          to Pippa, 11.8.91, Fawcett Library.

100 18   . . . the Secretary of a very important Committee—
          Information given by Baroness Stocks to the author.

100 26   "Who should turn up"—Dorothy to Pippa, 13.10.93,
          STP.

100 30   Once upon a time, in an effort to sustain—Information
          given by Duncan Grant to Michael Holroyd.

101 10   "the greatest chums"—Some Recollections/STP.

101 14   "But—but—but—"—"Kidnapped" from *Plain Tales
          from the Hills* (Kipling).

101 31   Apparently they just had enough—Information given
          by Duncan Grant to the author.

102   8   "He's rather trying"—Lytton to Duncan Grant (1906),
          quoted Holroyd, Vol. I.

102 24   he was seldom without his arm round Pippa's waist—
          Information given by Duncan Grant to the author.

102 28   "This is glory!"—Lady Strachey to Pippa, 30.5.07,
          STP.

103   9   "She made me feel, even as a child"—JMS/STP.

103 27   "How unfortunate it is"—Lytton to James, 9.5.09,
          quoted Holroyd, p. 438.

104   3   One of the most endearingly characteristic—Informa-
          tion given by Duncan Grant to the author. The
          story was told to D. G. by his housekeeper, Mrs
          Grace Higgens, to whom the incident actually
          occurred.

104 24   Virginia Woolf described the last time—JMS/STP.

235

TWO VICTORIAN FAMILIES

THE BENSONS

I

REFERENCES

Page Line

117　15　Fred's account of a similar occasion.—*Our Family Affairs*, p. 188.

118　3　"We were proud of my father"—*The Trefoil*, p. 51.

118　10　"the Lord Bishop of Truro"—*Our Family Affairs*, p. 59.

II

120　1　"We did not like Benson"—Recollections of Henry Richards, quoted in *History of Wellington College*.

120　10　"Her life was bound up"—*Life*, Vol. I, p. 144.

121　14　"More volatile"—*Mother* by E. F. Benson, p. 9.

122　15　"Let me try to recall"—E. W. Benson's Diary quoted in *As We Were* by E. F. Benson, p. 64.

123　21　"Mother rather feared than loved"—B/D 1/79.

126　4　"By the way you must remember"—E. W. Benson to Minnie Sidgwick, B/D 3/3.

126　13　"My dear Edward"—Minnie Sidgwick to E. W. Benson, B/D 3/3.

126　19　"According to his diary"—*As We Were*, p. 61.

127　5　"I love so dearly"—E. W. Benson to Minnie Sidgwick, B/D 3/15.

127　8　". . . a certain pillow"—Ibid.

127　18　"My own darling love"—Minnie Sidgwick to E. W. Benson, B/D 3/15.

127　28　"Wedding night"—B/D 1/79.

III

129　4　"I would have died"—B/D 1/79.

129　17　"a painful incident"—*History of Wellington College*.

129　23　"His work here did not prosper"—Recorded by the Rev. C. W. Penny, quoted in *Life*, Vol. I, p. 207.

REFERENCES

Page	Line	
138	19	"Miss Hall, the lady boarder"—Ibid., 26.7.72, B/D 3/3.
138	23	"Then I began to love Miss Hall"—B/D 1/79.
139	6	"It is far better"—Agnes Benson to E. W. Benson, 26.12.72, B/D 3/3.
139	14	"I am very much distressed"—Mrs Benson to E. W. Benson, B/D 3/3.
139	23	"I do try not to be more unhappy"—Ibid., 20.1.73, B/D 3/3.
140	1	"I haven't gone and I can't fully"—B/D 1/71.
140	17	"But," wrote Arthur Benson—*The Trefoil*, p. 78.
141	1	"I regarded him with awe"—Ibid., p. 116.
141	10	"He contrived to make me appear"—Ibid.
141	13	"He did me much good"—E. W. Benson's diary quoted in *Life*, Vol. II.
141	21	"How they felt it!"—B/D 1/79.
141	ftn.	He also had a sense of humour—*The Trefoil*, p. 117.
142	17	"Thou of thine abundant, rich goodness"—B/D 1/79.
142	24	"when I became a Christian"—B/D 1/79.
143	22	"I shall indeed as earnestly as I can"—E. W. Benson to Mrs Benson, 30.3.76, quoted in *Life*, Vol. I, pp. 396-8.
145	2	"for *harmonious* life"—B/D 1/79.

IV

146	9	"to the lengthy explanations"—*Life*, Vol. I, p. 18.
147	13	"I went for a lonely walk"—Mrs Benson's diary, 6.5.96, B/D 1/78.
147	25	On one occasion—*Life*, Vol. I, p. 442.
148	1	"I have been so very wretched"—Mrs Benson to Susan Wordsworth. Undated (1877), B/D 3/18.

REFERENCES

V

Page	Line	
155	ftn.	Henry Sidgwick apologised—Essay on Henry Sidgwick from *The Leaves of the Tree*, by A. C. Benson.
155	22	"Our little sheltered boy."—E. W. Benson's diary, 20.6.89, quoted in Martindale, p. 57.
156	ftn.	Martin and Arthur—*The Trefoil*, p. 85.
156	17	"a long, very affectionate"—Ibid., p. 59.
157	8	"how enormously and tremendously nicer"—Maggie to Mrs Benson, 1.2.94, quoted in *Maggie*, p. 168.
157	16	"rather a close little corporation"—*The Trefoil*, p. 258.
159	10	"well-known essays"—A. C. Benson to Geoffrey Madan, 18.8.14.
160	2	"I observed with a certain acuteness"—*Final Edition*, p. 182.
160	23	"going along quite independently"—Martindale, Vol. II, p. 311.
162	3	"Every corner was so full of ghosts"—A. C. Benson to Geoffrey Madan, 3.6.15.
163	5	"F. is insolent and quarrelsome"—Ibid., 29.12.16.
163	19	"double personality"—*Final Edition*, p. 21.
164	5	"Ride with Hugh"—E. F. Benson's diary, 21.11.87.
164	13	"he turned on Aunt Nora Sidgwick"—*Final Edition*, p. 33.
164	19	he bitterly resented an exasperated brother—Ibid., p. 34.
164	26	"In my books I am solemn, sweet, refined"—Diary, A. C. Benson, quoted in *Final Edition*, p. 24.
165	6	"Arthur goes round every night"—Mrs Benson to Maggie, 20.9.99, B/D 3/62.
165	11	"Arthur Benson was the only master"—*Life of Lord Halifax* by the Earl of Birkenhead, Chapter III.

Page Line
166   24   "GRACELESS MOTHER"—A. C. Benson to Mrs Benson, B/D 3/48.

166   26   "Composed a story yesterday"—Ibid., B/D 3/48.

167   6   "My own failing"—A. C. Benson's diary edited by Percy Lubbock, 27.6.13.

167   24   "Housman flicking cold water"—A. C. Benson to Geoffrey Madan, 6.2.24.

167   28   "A naked exhibition"—Ibid,. 18.7.15.

167   29   Lady Mount Temple "strangely attired"—Ibid., 11.5.14.

168   23   "I am not sure that yours strikes me"—*Our Family Affairs*, p. 282.

170   22   "The most remarkable thing about him"—*Hugh*, p. 37.

171   10   "We were all her children"—*Our Family Affairs*, p. 15.

171   17   "I am surprised at the intelligent interest"—E. W. Benson's Diary, 21.7.83, Wren Library.

VI

172   6   "swift, furious, baseless" moods—Mrs Benson to Maggie, 9.3.99, B/D 3/62.

172   7   Hugh . . . "too foolish"—Ibid., 11.3.99, B/D 3/62.

172   8   "Fred's mind is so inaccurate"—Ibid., B/D 3/62.

172   10   "I was going swimmingly along"—Ibid., 2.9.99, B/D 3/62.

172   18   "There is a delightful incident"—*Final Edition*, pp. 101-4.

173   15   the "awful inner tie"—Mrs Benson to Ethel Smyth, 26.3.89, B/D 3/3.

173   19   "Mother . . . do you know the thought of you"—Maggie Benson to Mrs Benson, 1885, quoted in *Maggie*, p. 67.

REFERENCES

Page Line

174 10 She realised, she wrote, that "in one sense"—Nellie Benson's diary quoted by A. C. Benson in his preface to her novel. *In Sundry Times and in Divers Manners.*

174 18 "There was a mood"—*Maggie*, p. 117.

175 7 "It seems too great a happiness"—Ethel Matthews to Nellie Benson, B/D 3/59.

175 27 "from 1886 onwards"—*Impressions that Remained* by Dame Ethel Smyth, Vol. II, p. 188.

175 30 "in deadlier awe"—Ibid., Vol. II, p. 191.

176 1 "eventually became my particular friend"—Ibid., Vol. II, p. 190.

176 6 "Think over the past"—Mrs Benson to Ethel Smyth, 26.10.89, B/D 3/38. The original of this letter is not to be traced among the Benson papers but it is one of several typed copies of letters written to various female correspondents (chiefly Mrs Mandell Creighton and the latter's daughter, Gemma Bailey). These letters may loosely be described as offering 'soul guidance' and someone at one time obviously had the idea of making a book of them, presumably for private circulation. The project was, perhaps wisely, abandoned.

177 23 "pale and smiling through her tears"—*Maggie*, p. 115.

178 2 "It appears to me"—Ethel Matthews to Nellie Benson, B/D 59/2.

178 15 "My work is awfully nice this term"—Maggie Benson to Mrs Benson, 1885, *Maggie*, p. 68.

179 3 "That wretched 'Women's' Examination—Ibid., p. 122.

180 2 "for the first time almost"—Maggie Benson to Mrs Benson, 1894, *Maggie*, p. 116.

180 13 "The only thing I should like more of"—Maggie Benson to Mrs Benson, 1.12.94, *Maggie*, p. 168.

REFERENCES

Page Line

187 12 "O Maggie"—Mrs Benson to Maggie, 12.2.93, B/D 3/60.

188 ftn. She once complained—Mrs Benson's diary, undated, B/D 1/77.

188 10 "Meggie . . . and Lucy are delightful companions"— E. W. Benson's diary, 18.8.92, Wren Library.

188 12 "Lucy Tait, who not only thinks"—Ibid., 15.5.94, Wren Library.

188 ftn. "A discussion has been raging downstairs"—Maggie Benson to Nettie Gourlay, 1896, *Maggie*.

188 20 "it is impossible to think of them apart"—*Final Edition* by E. F. Benson, p. 13.

188 22 "Lucy slept with my mother"—Ibid., p. 16.

189 27 "O Maggie, Arthur on the Box Seat"—Mrs Benson to Maggie, 21.2 (probably 1899), B/D 3/62.

189 30 "A great step has been made"—Mrs Benson to Hugh, 12.1.99, B/D 3/72.

189 34 "his very personality"—*Final Edition*, p. 11.

190 9 "Maggie plunged in deep gloom"—Mrs Benson's diary, 1898, B/D 1/78.

190 18 "M. and I"—Ibid., B/D 1/78.

190 25 "What am I to do?"—Ibid., B/D 1/78.

191 7 "a long vista of slavery"—Ibid., B/D 1/78.

191 19 "A terrible talk with Maggie"—Ibid., 8.11.99, B/D 1/78.

192 5 "Once more with shame"—Ibid., B/D 1/78.

192 11 "It still remains as it ever did"—Ibid., B/D 1/78.

192 27 "In the country"—*Mother*, pp. 82-3.

192 31 "I am utterly ashamed"—Mrs Benson's diary, 20.7.88, B/D 1/78.

193 19 ". . . that fatal knife"—Sonnet 50 from *Modern Love* by George Meredith.

Page	Line	
193	21	"My dear & precious Person"—Mrs Benson to Maggie, 28.10.02, B/D 3/62.
194	16	"an exhaustive letter"—Mrs Benson's diary, 5.6.99, B/D 1/78.
195	1	"his manservant"—Mrs Benson to Maggie, 30.12.00, B/D 3/61.
195	15	As a schoolboy—E. W. Benson to J. B. Lightfoot, 5.7.48, quoted in *Life*, Vol. II, p. 62.
195	22	"It is not too much to say"—*Life*, Vol. II, p. 582.
196	19	E. F. Benson says—*Mother*, p. 253.
197	4	"Lucy and I compared the 2 services"—Mrs Benson's diary, 13.6.03, B/D 1/78.

VIII

Page	Line	
198	9	"You must get your mother's permission"—*Final Edition*, p. 30.
198	17	"Fred playing with his Earls and Countesses"—Mrs Benson to Maggie Benson, 28.5.00, B/D 3/72.
199	3	"Oh I am killing it!"—*Mother*, p. 222.
199	12	"no longer ... like a piece of old and frayed elastic"—Maggie Benson to A. C. Benson, 3.5.06, *Maggie*, p. 357.
199	14	"Oh it's perfect here"—Maggie Benson to R. H. Benson, 20.5.06, *Maggie*, p. 305.
199	28	"I believe the mists will disperse"—Maggie Benson to A. C. Benson, 19.3.07, *Maggie*, p. 386.
200	4	She also called on her brother Fred—*Mother*, p. 225.
200	8	it "was prettier"—Maggie Benson to Gladys Bevan, 30.5.07, *Maggie*, p. 389.
200	14	"The world assumed to her"—*Mother*, p. 225.
200	19	"He persuaded her to act normally"—*Mother*, p. 221.

REFERENCES

Page	Line	
201	4	. . . a young guest of Arthur's—Information given to the author by Mrs Geoffrey Madan.
201	15	"It is very difficult, Dearest"—Mrs Benson to Maggie Benson, 28.11.02, B/D 3/62.
201	22	E. F. Benson wrote—*Final Edition*, p. 135.
201	28	One letter survives—Mrs Benson to Maggie Benson, B/D 3/62.
201	13	Arthur and Hugh had formed a close friendship—*Final Edition*, p. 165.
201	20	"In one way this odd outburst"—Maggie Benson to A. C. Benson, 22.5.06, *Maggie*, p. 359.
202	2	"Her memory was absolutely unimpaired"—*Mother*, pp. 244-5.

IX

205	15	"For six whole years"—A. C. Benson to Geoffrey Madan, 2.5.23.
205	23	David Newsome attributes—*Godliness and Good Learning*, p. 193.
206	2	He himself compared it—R. H. Benson to Mrs Lieblich, 1914, quoted in Martindale, Vol. II.
206	6	"His brain was as restless as ever"—Martindale, Vol. II, p. 426.
206	24	R.H.B. in his last moments—Arthur Benson's Note Book in the possession of John Gere.
206	32	"the Thing was there"—*Up and Down*, p. 123.
208	13	"quite unconceivable"—*Confessions of a Convert*, p. 29.
208	19	The one supreme happiness of my life just now—A. C. Benson's diary, ed. Percy Lubbock, 7.12.10.
208	23	"I'm a little anxious"—Letter to Geoffrey Madan, 4.2.15.

TWO VICTORIAN FAMILIES

REFERENCES

Page Line

217 18 "natural priesthood of women"—"Priests", an essay in *From a College Window*, by A. C. Benson.

217 ftn. "Mrs Benson used actually"—*Bright Morning* by Constance Sitwell, p. 50.

217 25 "Her master passion"—*Impressions that Remained* by Ethel Smyth, Vol. II, p. 188.

218 10 Maggie "never shrank"—*Maggie*, p. 146.

218 30 He "had quite a definite opinion"—Martindale, Vol. II, p. 237, footnote 2.

219 11 "Just at present I am like Pentheus"—A. C. Benson to Geoffrey Madan, 5.3.15.

219 14 "In dealing with Hugh's affairs"—Ibid., 17.5.15.

219 16 "I was engaged all yesterday"—Ibid., 30.1.15.

219 27 "I have become the beloved author"—Arthur Benson's Diary, 27.6.13.

219 31 A very typical letter—A. C. Benson to J. Ewing, 5.7.11. In the possession of Dr Ewing.

222 3 The Archbishop once thanked Heaven—E. W. Benson's diary, 8.6.96, Wren Library.

222 6 "I suppose we all have a touch of something morbid" —A. C. Benson's diary, 27.6.13.

BIBLIOGRAPHY

Benson, A. C., *Life of Edward White Benson, Archbishop of Canterbury* (2 vols.), Macmillan & Co., 1899.

——, *The Leaves of the Tree*, Smith Elder & Co., 1913.

——, *Hugh*, Smith Elder & Co., 1915.

——, *Life and Letters of Maggie Benson*, John Murray, 1917.

——, *The Trefoil*, John Murray, 1923.

——, *Diary*, edited by Percy Lubbock, Hutchinson, 1926.

——, Memoir of M. E. (Nellie) Benson, published as a preface to her novel *In Sundry Times and in Divers Manners*, Kegan Paul, 1891.

Benson, E. F., *Up and Down*, Hutchinson, 1919.

——, *Our Family Affairs*, Cassell & Co., 1920.

——, *Mother*, Hodder & Stoughton, 1925.

——, *As We Were*, Longmans, 1930.

——, *Final Edition*, Longmans, 1940.

Benson, R. H., *Confessions of a Convert*, Longmans, 1913.

Birkenhead, Earl of, *Life of the Third Earl of Halifax*, Hamish Hamilton, 1965.

Chinna Durai, J, *The Choice before India*, Jonathan Cape 1941.

Fothergill, Brian, "A Friendship's Downfall" included in *New Quests for Corvo*, Icon Books Ltd., 1965.

Hassall, Christopher, *Rupert Brooke*, Faber & Faber, 1964.

Holroyd, Michael, *Lytton Strachey* (2 vols.), Heinemann, 1967.

——, *Lytton Strachey By Himself* (ed. Holroyd), Heinemann, 1971.

BIBLIOGRAPHY

Martindale, Father, *Life of Monsignor Robert Hugh Benson* (2 vols.) Longmans, 1916.

Newsome, David, *History of Wellington College*, John Murray, 1961.

——, *Godliness and Good Learning*, Jonathan Cape, 1941.

Rolfe, F, *The Desire and Pursuit of the Whole*, Cassell & Co., 1934.

Sitwell, Constance, *Bright Morning*, Jonathan Cape, 1942.

Smyth, Ethel, *Impressions That Remained* (2 vols.), Longmans, 1919.

Strachey, Dorothy, *Olivia*, Hogarth Press, 1951.

Symons, A. J. A., *The Quest for Corvo*, Cassell & Co., 1935.

Woolf, Leonard, *Sowing*, Hogarth Press, 1960.

——, *The Journey not the Arrival Matters*, Hogarth Press, 1969.

INDEX

Part One—The Stracheys

INDEX

INDEX

Strachey, Elinor—*contd.*

57; shares the family talent for the written word, 57-58; paired with Dick, 58; at Mlle Souvestre's school, 59; on her mother's love of her family, 97, 103

Strachey, James:

at home, 18, 26; a letter from his father, 34-35, 50; at Rugby, 39, 40; becomes a 'conchie', 1914, 44-45; 'Uncle Baby', 55-56, 57, 58, 69, 75; a struggle with Marjorie, 74; Cambridge friends, 96; studies psychoanalysis in Vienna, 104

Strachey, John (Sir Richard's brother): serves in India, 29; Commissioner to the Central Provinces, 36, 80, 88n; disapproves of Nellie, 88; a visit from Pippa, 92

Strachey, Julia (Oliver's daughter), 51

Strachey, Lytton:

on No. 69 Lancaster Gate, 18, 26, 28; about the family wine, 19; describes the butlers, 22-23; Hugo's *Notre Dame*, 25; a delicate boy, 27, 40; at Liverpool, 39; affected by his mother's lack of temperament, 44, 46; on Dorothy's engagement, 44; a 'conchie', 44-45; measles at school, 47; his 'Strachey' voice, 48; a light hearted, lively boy, 51-52; his homosexuality, 52-53, 54; his relationship with Duckworth, 52; his affection for Pippa, 53, 54; many illnesses, 53, 54, 55n, 66; sends for Pippa in Paris, 54; his personal troubles, 54-55, 56; caricatures Mlle Schaller, 56; pairs with Marjorie, 58, 74-75; skating with Pippa, 69; a gifted and brilliant child, 75; Cambridge friends, 96; Sunday afternoon

at Lancaster Gate, 97-98; Uncle Trevor's eating habits, 102; in praise of Pippa, 103; lives in the country, 103-104; see also *Eminent Victorians*; *Ermyntrude and Esmerelda*

Strachey, Marjorie:

at home, 23, 26; on her mother at Lancaster Gate, 18-19, 20; a poor housekeeper, 22; at Allenswood, 39, 42, 61; affected by her mother's lack of sensuality, 44, 73; her massiveness, 47n, 66, 74, 76; educated at Mlle Souvestre's, 51; her birth, 55; on her sister, Elinor, 57; pairs with Lytton, 58, 74-75; her childhood and life, 73-77; an unfortunate position in the family, 75; not intellectually distinguished, 75-77; an affair with Colonel J. Wedgwood, 77n; a violin from Uncle Trevor, 102; quarrels with her mother, 103

Strachey, Oliver: in the Traffic Department, 34-35, 50, 79; sent down from Balliol, 45, 45n, 49-50; the bicycle incident, 48; on Ralph's future wife, 49; his career and marriage, 50-51, 78, 81 a strange letter from Lytton, 53; a poem, 58; pairs with Pernel, 58; writes to Pippa, 66; a visit from Pippa, 91-92

Strachey, Mrs Oliver, *see* Mayer, Ruby

Strachey, Olivia, 58

Strachey, Pernel:

a friend of Simon Bussy, 25, 64; at Cambridge, 34, 39, 72-71; diphtheria in Yorkshire, 40; top in her French examinations, 49; educated at Mlle Souvestre's, 51, 61; pairs with Oliver, 58; on Dorothy's depression, 61; relationship with Pippa, 66, 70,

INDEX

71; appearance, 66, 73; in the Bach choir, Cambridge, 71; Principal of Newnham, 1923, 73, 104; teaches at Royal Holloway College, 75; an educated, independent and self-sufficient woman, 77; delights in Aunt Hennie's comments, 100; a 'wee bookcase' from Uncle Trevor, 102

Strachey, Philippa:
in Scotland, 21, 39; housekeeper for her mother, 21-22; at dinner, 20n; on the drains, 25; a bilious attack, 25; at parties, 27, 32-33; in India, 35-36, 47-48, 78-94, 102; weekly money to the Reservist families, 45; on family appearances, 47; a sister-in-law-like comment, 48; the bicycle incident, 48; her relationship with Lytton, 51, 53, 66; letters to my dearest 'Folderol', 51-52; on Lytton's illnesses, 55n; not uncritical of Jimbeau, 56; pairs with Ralph, 58, 66; friendship with Dorothy, 62-63, 66, 70; the family prop, 66; her appearance, 66-67; her beaux, 67-69; friendship with the Croalls, 69; fond of sports, 69-70; her dearest sister, 70-71; plays a recorder then a contrabass viol, 71; an independent and self-sufficient woman, 77, 78-79; Secretary of the Fawcett Society and women's rights, 79, 104; her love for India, 80; illness and an accident, 80-82; on Arthur Strachey, 81; in mourning for Queen Victoria, 82; with the East India Railway, 82-83; a visit to the Frontier, 83; takes charge of Arthur's cremation and affairs, 83-88; Azerat Ram and her rickshaw, 88-90, 91, 93; a

week in the hills, 89-90; at Ralph's wedding, 90-91; a tourist's round, 91; prefers Ruby to Margaret, 91-92; her return via Florence, 92-93; meets Huxley, 95-96; on Aunt Lell, 98-99; Uncle Trevor's favourite, 102; behaves with decency and propriety, 103

Strachey, Ralph: his career and place in the family, 49, 58, 66, 79; a visit from Pippa, 78, 81, 82-83; his marriage, 90-91, 92; knowledge of Indian vernacular, 93

Strachey, Sir Richard:
his study, 20; at meals, 20n, 22, 32; his health, 24-25, 31, 33; buys Bussy's painting, 25-26, 64; at soirées, 26-27; his career and marriage, 29-36; old age and his deafness, 31-36; his Royal medal, 1897, 30, 70; his relationship with his family, 32-36, 50; Indian service, 29, 31, 36-37, 80; his G.C.S.I., 39; buys Dorothy and Bussy a villa, 65; retires without a pension, 71; pride at Pernel's entry to Newnham, 72; at the Athenæum with Pippa and Huxley, 95-96; his death, 1908, 103

Strachey, William: his eccentricity, 98, 100-101

Strachey family, the: Anglo-Indian roots, 29-31, 36-38, 78-94, 105; appearance, 47, 66, 71, 74; aunts and uncles, 100-3, 105; clannishness and family feeling, 49; croquet, 69; distinguished friends, 95; illness, 24-25, 40; meals and conversation, 19-20, 20n, 21, 22, 32; music, 105; parties, 26-27, 32-33; their servants, 19, 20-24, 25, 40, 104; Ellen, a devoted servant, 24, 33-34, 56; the 'Strachey voice', 47-48

INDEX

Part Two—The Bensons

INDEX

INDEX

little boy, 170-171; his foolish-
ness, 172; not friendly with
Fred, 173, 202; his mother
cancels a visit, 191; becomes a
Roman Catholic, 195-197; uses
the Tremans chapel for Mass,
198; a compulsive writer, 205-
206; his dislike of women, 208,
212; a 'disastrous intimacy',
213-217; his lady penitents,
218-220
Writings: 158, 160-161, 202
The Coward, 161-162
An Average Man, 161
The Necromancers, 161
Confessions of a Convert, 161
The Light Invisible, 172
The Sentimentalists: Chris Dell,
214-215, 217
Initiation: Enid Bessington, 214-
217
Benson, Maggie:
under the cedar tree, 117;
hears of her father's appoint-
ment to Truro, 118; her birth,
1865, 132; confides her troubles,
133; at Lady Margaret Hall,
157; committed to an asylum,
170, 200, 222; her mother's
fondness for her, 173, 179, 187;
shielded and helped by Nellie,
177; a brilliant Oxford career,
178-179; her ill-health, 179, 187;
visits to Athens and Egypt,
179-180, 181, 187; character
and appearance, 177, 179, 181;
friendship with Nettie Gourlay,
181, 208; her relationship with
L.J., 181-182, 207, 208; a
Queen at a garden party, 183;
scornful of Lucy's intellectual
abilities, 188, 188n; the 'cult'
of her father, 189-190; her
jealousy of Lucy, 189, 191-192,
199, 200, 200n; helps with the
official *Life*, 189, 193, 195n;
develops her father's black
moods, 190, 193, 198-200;

causes the family to move to
Tremans, 193; at Tremans, 193-
194, 198-200; friendship with
Gladys Bevan, 194, 208; homicidal mania 200, 200n; an
unexpected visitor, 200-201;
taken out by Arthur, 202;
returns to her early closeness to
Fred, 202-204; ill-health and
periods of normality, 203-204;
her death, 204; on Hugh's
religion, 213; keen on advising
others, 218
Writings: 157-158; *The Venture
of Rational Faith*, 157-158, 194;
edits her father's *Revelations*, 189
Benson, Martin White: his father's
favourite child, 118; his birth,
1860, 132, more like a brother
than a son, 133; his life and
death, 149-151; 151n; the effect
of his death on his family, 151-
155, 177; his possible future,
155; an attack of vertigo, 156n;
his place in his family, 166-167;
manic depressive moods, 205;
prepared his sisters for confirmation, 218
Benson, Nellie: asleep under the
cedar tree, 117; her birth, 1863,
132; letters to Martin, 150; her
writings, 157; her character
and resemblance to her mother,
174-175; her black moods, 174,
205; friendship with Ethel
Smyth, 176, 208; her death and
its affect on the family, 177,
179; the least afraid of E. W.
Benson after Martin, 177, 189;
called home from Lady
Margaret Hall, 177; her interest
in social work at Lambeth, 178
Benson family, the: at Kenwyn,
146-147; a sheltered life, 155-
157, 207; great writers of books,
157-162; enchained by their
past, 162; family games, 162,
177; the place of the girls in the

261

INDEX

262

INDEX

Rolfe, Fr.: his friendship and quarrel with Hugh, 213-217; his writings, *The Desire and Pursuit of the Whole*—Monsignor Bobugo Bonson, 214-215, 217

Sidgwick, Mrs: settles in Rugby, 121; bulldozed into giving her permission, 122; her relationship with Minnie, 123-125; has Edward and Minnie to stay, 129; 'an unhappy visit', 131

Sidgwick, Arthur: a visit to Wellington, 132; sends Minnie to Germany, 137

Sidgwick, Henry: founder of the Society for Physical Research, 127; a visit to Wellington, 132; apologies to Arthur Benson, 155n

Sidgwick, Minnie, *see* Benson, Mrs

Sitwell, Constance: hears Mrs Benson speak, 217n

Smyth, Ethel (the composer): a friend of Nellie's, 175-176, 208; on Mrs Benson's master passion, 217-218

Society for Psychical Research, 121, 121n

Tait, Lucy: an emotional relationship with Mrs Benson, 134, 188-189, 191-192, 199, 200, 204, 212; moves into the Benson household, 184, 188; her background and character, 187-189; on Mrs Benson and her family, 188n; not very intellectual, 188, 188n; compares the ordination services, 197

Temple, Lady Mount, 167-168, 167n

Tennant, Margot: a fictional portrait, 168-169

Tremans, Horsted Keyes, 193, 198-200

Truro Cathedral, 148-149

Truro Diocese, 146-148

Victoria, Queen: a mid-Victorian, 109

Vincent, Marlborough friend of E. F. Benson's, 211

Walker, Agnes (Mrs C. Benson): her marriage to Christopher, 137; writes home for Minnie, 139

Warre, Doctor: wants Benson to stand for headmastership of Eton, 165

Wellington College, 109, 111-113, 120, 129

Winchester, 192-193, 194

Winchester Cathedral: an epitaph to Martin, 153, 153n

Winchester School: Martin as a pupil, 149, 151

Wordsworth, Christopher: Bishop of Lincoln, 135; relationship with E. W. Benson, 135, 137, 140

Wordsworth, Elizabeth, 135-136, 147, 156

Wordsworth family, the: friends of the Benson family, 135-136, 147

Yeats Brown, Francis, 211, 211n

Yonge, Charlotte Mary, 116